THE LAST MINUTE

A STUDY OF THE INTERTESTAMENTAL PERIOD

STEVEN C. HUNTER

ISBN 978-1-944704-24-7

Published by Start2Finish
Bend, Oregon 97702
start2finish.org

Printed in the United States of America

Cover Design: Evangela Creative

CONTENTS

PREFACE

The historical period between Malachi and Matthew has long been a subject of interest for serious Bible students. When one transitions from the Old to the New Testament, several changes take place. Where did Herod, the Romans, and the Pharisees come from? What about Hanukkah and the Apocrypha?

In Galatians 4:4, Paul asserts that God sent his Son into the world at just the right moment—"the fullness of time." Look at any calendar and it's evident that the Advent of the Messiah was the climax of history in more ways than one. The 400 years of history before Jesus' birth, therefore, represent "the last minute" in God's scheme of redemption.

In this study, Steven Hunter takes the student on a tour through the political, cultural, and religious transformations that took place between Malachi and Matthew. Given his love and study of both classical history and the Scriptures, I can think of no one I'd rather have as my guide through this particular epoch than Steven.

— Michael Whitworth

ACKNOWLEDGMENTS

I am greatly indebted to the following works that have helped me in my research on the Intertestamental Period:

- Ferguson, Everett. *Backgrounds of Early Christianity*. 3d. ed. (Grand Rapids: Wm. B. Eerdmans Publishing Company, 2003)
- Scott, J. Julius. *Jewish Backgrounds of the New Testament*. (Grand Rapids: Baker Academic, 1995)
- Surburg, Raymond F. *Introduction to the Intertestamental Period*. (St. Louis: Concordia Publishing House, 1975)

Many of the lessons herein benefited from these three works, and since many of my lessons here were originally in outline form when I made this work, I'm hard-pressed to identify where I might have borrowed the work of these scholars in my lessons. Suffice it to say, their scholarship has aided the production of this work, and I thank them for their scholarship and what I've gleaned from them.

1

INTRODUCTION TO THE INTERTESTAMENTAL PERIOD

The narrative of God's people didn't stop upon the completion of the Old Testament. God's work among His people didn't simply have a gap in time. However, we do lack the certainty of divine revelation between a period of about 400 years that spans between the completion of the Old Testament and the time of events in the New Testament that begins with the visitation of the angel to Zacharias. I hope to fill in some of the gaps in our knowledge of that time period as a way to better link our Old and New Testament, as well as to help us better understand our New Testament given that things mentioned in them aren't referred to in the Old Testament. Hopefully, you'll find this to be as edifying a study as I would desire it to be.

A PRELUDE

The Intertestamental Period is the time period between the end of Malachi and the beginning of Matthew. It's referred to this way because it's the time between the testaments of the Bible. At the closing of the Old Testament, the Jews lived under Persian rule. However, the

Greeks would arise to conquer the Persians, and then the Romans would prevail over the Greeks to become the world's superpower. All of this was foretold in Nebuchadnezzar's dream in Daniel 2.

> This is the dream. Now we will tell the interpretation of it before the king. You, O king, are a king of kings. For the God of heaven has given you a kingdom, power, strength, and glory; and wherever the children of men dwell, or the beasts of the field and the birds of the heaven, He has given them into your hand, and has made you ruler over them all—you are this head of gold. But after you shall arise another kingdom inferior to yours; then another, a third kingdom of bronze, which shall rule over all the earth. And the fourth kingdom shall be as strong as iron, inasmuch as iron breaks in pieces and shatters everything; and like iron that crushes, that kingdom will break in pieces and crush all the others. Whereas you saw the feet and toes, partly of potter's clay and partly of iron, the kingdom shall be divided; yet the strength of the iron shall be in it, just as you saw the iron mixed with ceramic clay. And as the toes of the feet were partly of iron and partly of clay, so the kingdom shall be partly strong and partly fragile. As you saw iron mixed with ceramic clay, they will mingle with the seed of men; but they will not adhere to one another, just as iron does not mix with clay. (Daniel 2:36–43)

The book of Nehemiah was the last to be written in the Old Testament, and it dates to 424–400 B.C. The book of James is believed to have been the earliest writing of the New Testament and dates to A.D. 44–49. Between those dates, a lot of history occurred that we don't have in our Bibles.

Between the testaments is an entire body of writings we refer to as the Apocrypha that tells much of the history that occurred in this time period. Moreover, in the New Testament we read about the synagogue, Pharisees, and Sadducees—none of which are mentioned in the Old Testament. Knowing our Intertestamental Period history can better aid our understanding of the New Testament.

GOD'S SILENCE

The silence of God through the prophets is notable in the Intertestamental Period. God had spoken by the prophets to His people for centuries (Hosea 12:10). The first prophet ever mentioned was Abraham, the father of both Judaism and Christianity (Genesis 20:7). Many of our Old Testament prophets were literary, but others were not. Abraham, Nathan, Elijah, and Elisha were prophets who never penned a book. Later, John the Baptist was also a non-literary prophet.

Reflecting back over the history of God's people, Nehemiah acknowledged that God had indeed spoken to His people through the prophets (Nehemiah 9:30). Before that time, Amos had stated that God did nothing unless He disclosed it to His prophets (Amos 3:7). Yet, God promised that a day would come when the prophets would be silent.

"Behold, the days are coming," says the Lord God, "That I will send a famine on the land, Not a famine of bread, Nor a thirst for water, But of hearing the words of the Lord. They shall wander from sea to sea, And from north to east; They shall run to and fro, seeking the word of the Lord, But shall not find it." (Amos 8:11–12)

A particular Psalm dated to decades after 586 B.C. expressed the widespread pain of having been chastised by God. In Psalm 74, the psalmist noted the absence of the prophetic voice as feeling like God had abandoned them, "There is no longer any prophet" (Psalm 74:9). Of course, history tells us that the prophets again spoke after the Babylonian exile which occurred in 586 B.C. Whether Amos' prophecy was reflected in the Psalm or if it pointed to this particular period is unknown, but a case can be made either way. Yet, contextually, Amos' prophecy indeed looks more toward the Assyrian captivity which took place before the Babylonian captivity. Nevertheless, one might also argue that a greater meaning is to be found in Amos' words just as the writers of the New Testament found higher meanings in passages that, on the surface, were not Messianic, but that they later identified as such.

Whatever the case was, Malachi urged Israel to pay close attention to the Law of Moses (Malachi 4:4). Even absent a contemporary prophet, the Mosaic Law certainly was adequate enough to guide the people in righteousness and holiness. And the Word did just that during the tumultuous period between the testaments as will later be shown.

Suffice it to say, we do have Intertestamental evidence that there was a common belief that the prophets were silent.

> So they tore down the altar, and stored the stones in a convenient place on the temple hill until a prophet should come to tell what to do with them. (1 Maccabees 4:45b–46 NRSV)

> So there was great distress in Israel, such as had not been since the time that prophets ceased to appear among them. (1 Maccabees 9:27)

The Jews and their priests have resolved that Simon should be their leader and high priest forever, until a trustworthy prophet should arise. (1 Maccabees 14:41)

The book of 1 Maccabees covers the events that happened in Palestine from 175–134 B.C., and the book claims to have been written around 100 B.C. The author(s) of 1 Maccabees believed that there was not a reliable prophet in their time and that there had not been one for some time. It might be totally unfair to assume that the writer believes this to have applied to the entirety of what we call the Intertestamental Period because they actually—in the last passage cited—were looking for a reliable prophet to arise in their time. It is unknown whether there was or wasn't. However, what we must be fair to state is that the absence of prophets didn't necessarily mean the lack of divine inspiration. After all, the writer of Psalm 74 lacked prophets, but his Psalm is included among the inspired writings. For other reasons to be explored in a future lesson, we do not believe the Apocrypha to be divinely inspired, though it is rather historically reliable.

THE LESSONS

You might have been startled to learn that Nehemiah was the last book to be written and that James was the first in their respective testaments. After all, Malachi is listed last and Matthew is listed first. This study will require something of you—and that's that you not be frightened by information that challenges what you've always believed. There's actually much wisdom in this statement—"The first one to plead his cause seems right, Until his neighbor comes and examines him" (Proverbs 18:17). It's true that the gospel accounts in our New Testaments begin with events that predate James' writing, but they were not actually composed in the order that they appear. This fact does nothing to challenge the inspiration or validity of God's Word. It's merely a fact of textual transmission. I'd say that the first lesson to keep in mind when studying this time period is not to be shocked at what you might learn. If you find yourself shocked or bothered, ask if what you've learned does anything to shake the foundation of your faith. You'll find that it more than likely doesn't. I'll do my best to explain how it doesn't along the way, but I may miss something here or there.

The second lesson I want to leave with you is one that Malachi left the Jews at the close of his prophecy—we, like them, must rely on the inspired Word that we have. Malachi was a prophet, but even he pointed the Jews to God's Word—to Moses' Law. This fact is telling in that even in the face of prophecy—which usually served a purpose for the time in which it was given—the foundation of God's Word was to be followed. This, after all, is what the prophets pointed the people to—scriptural fidelity. Though they were present in the New Testament church, you and I lack the apostles and prophets in our own day, so we should rely on the Word of God as our guide in all matters of faith. This information on this time period that I'll share with you isn't divinely inspired, but it can be helpful to us as Bible students. Therefore, I'll give you a piece of advice given to me by one of my teachers, "Eat the fish and throw away the bone." There are good things to be found in books, so take the good and leave the bad. Never allow what may be complex to overrule what is simplistic. Never allow what is secular to guide you in contradiction to what is sacred.

FILL IN THE BLANK

1. The Jews were under _____ rule at the end of the Old Testament.

2. The _____ would conquer the Persians, and the _____ would conquer the Greeks.

3. The last book written in the Old Testament was _____ while the earliest New Testament writing was _____.

4. We don't read about _____ and _____ in our Old Testaments, but we do read about them in our New Testaments.

5. The book of _____ suggests that there hadn't been a prophet in much of the Intertestamental Period.

DISCUSSION QUESTIONS

1. Since 1 Maccabees is not inspired, how can we even trust it when it says that there were no prophets during the Intertestamental Period? Is that not choosing which data suits our beliefs?

2. What can you say about the Intertestamental Period as a focus of study for better understanding the New Testament?

3. How might Daniel's prophecy have been understood as those living in the Intertestamental Period saw the unraveling of those very events? Do you think they knew them at that time? Why or why not? Think about how well we understand revelation when discussing this question.

4. "Never allow what is secular to guide you in contradiction to what is sacred." Discuss areas where people have allowed secular information to lead them away from what the Bible says.

5. Discuss the arrangement of the order of the books of the Bible. Would it be helpful to consider the events in chronological order rather than by book arrangement? What are some benefits to the book order we currently have in the Bible?

2

THE RISE OF THE GREEKS

Our Old Testaments are primarily concerned with the ancient Near East, so we often fail to realize what was happening in other parts of the world during the same time period as the biblical events we are studying. Many of us know some of the events of western civilization from a class taken in high school and college, but we may not realize how those events line up with events in Scripture. However, when it comes to the Intertestamental Period, Grecian history becomes important to us as people of faith to help us better understand this time period. The Greek historian Herodotus estimated that the poet Homer lived in the ninth century B.C.—contemporary to 1 & 2 Samuel, Obadiah, and possibly Joel—and wrote his masterpieces, *Iliad*, and *Odyssey*, during that time. Greece's history spans a longer time than what we might think.

FROM PERSIA TO GREECE

At the close of the Old Testament, the Persian rulers had allowed the Jews to return to Jerusalem to rebuild what the Babylonians had destroyed—the city and the Temple (cf. 2 Chronicles 36:20; Isaiah 44:28; Jeremiah 51:11; Ezra 1:1–4). God had foretold through Isaiah that the Persians, or Medes, would be stirred up against the Babylonians (Isaiah 13:17), but even Persian rule wouldn't last forever. After two hundred years of Palestinian inhabitance under the Persians, a new force emerged that would defeat the Persian rule, the Greeks.

What may escape many Bible students' notice is that though the Greeks are not mentioned too much in the Old Testament (cf. Joel 3:6; Daniel 8:21; 10:20; 11:2; Zechariah 9:13), history informs us that they were thriving during Old Testament times. For example, between chapters one and two of the book of Esther, the Persians had attempted to conquer the Greeks for the second time but were defeated. The king of Persia in Esther—Ahasuerus—is referred to by the Greeks as Xerxes. Historically, he's Xerxes I. Persia had tried to conquer Greece in two invasions—the first was from 492–490 B.C., within a decade or two of when Zechariah was written (480–470 B.C.). During this time, Sparta and Athens were the largest Greek city-states. The first invasion ended with an Athenian victory at the Battle of Marathon. Our modern conception of running a marathon (26 miles) derives from this Greek victory. According to Lucian (A.D. 125–180), the legend tells us that, upon Greece's victory, Philippides ran the entire distance to Athens to announce that they'd won. Upon giving his message, Philippides is said to have fallen dead.

The second invasion, led by Xerxes I (Ahasuerus), took place from 480–479 B.C. It was during this invasion that the infamous Battle of Thermopylae took place where 300 Spartans stood at a narrow pass fighting Persians for three days until reinforcements arrived. King Leonidas led his 300 Spartans, 700 Thespians, and 400 Thebans before a force of 7,000 came to aid them. While most of his force died at the narrow pass, they bought enough time for the Greeks to come so that they could defeat the Persians—something remarkable in their time given the notoriety of the Persian Empire.

PHILIP'S SON

Philip of Macedon (382–336 B.C.) accomplished the formation of a united government in Greece. Previously, Greece existed in city-states that the Persian kings were able to manipulate; however, because of their lack of unity, the Persians were able to suppress Greek hopes of being an offensive power in the world. However, after the two invasions of Persians upon Greek soil, Philip achieved the task of uniting Greece into a super power that would later dethrone Persia. Not all Greeks looked kindly upon this unity, though, because Macedonians were not seen as Greeks, but as barbarians. The Greeks referred to all non-Greeks as barbarians, just as the Jews referred to all non-Jews as Gentiles. Nevertheless, Philip was able to do something that hadn't been done before, and the Macedonians were eventually viewed as Greek because of this unification. Since Greece's strength was proven when they were united against the Persians, Philip was able to use this recent history to plead his case for a united Greece as opposed to one that consisted of city-states governed by their own kings.

Philip retained a high esteem of Greek culture, and so his son, Alexander the Great, was educated by the finest advocates of Greek culture. Alexander learned at the feet of the most notable philosopher of his time—Aristotle. Before young Alexander's tutelage under Aristotle, Symmachus instructed him in Homer's *Iliad*. Alexander grew to hold an admiration for all things Greek just as his father had. This zeal for Hellenism led Alexander to spread the culture as he conquered, but when he encountered God-fearing Jews, he refrained from imposing his culture on them because of a dream he supposedly had. Alexander's father was assassinated by one of his guards while he was attending a wedding, and so Alexander became king while he was a youth. The Macedonian army and noblemen declared Alexander their new king, and the new king would begin a conquest that included a stop in Palestine.

ALEXANDER'S ARRIVAL IN PALESTINE

By the time Alexander's army had arrived in Palestine, Persia was fading quickly. When Alexander left Macedon, his aim was to defeat the Persians. En route to Persia, his attention turned to the Eastern Mediterranean.

Sidon, Byblos, and Aradus submitted to the Greeks, but Tyre only fell after seven months of siege. Gaza also refused to surrender, so the army besieged the city with a harsher attitude than they previously had for Tyre. When Alexander arrived in Jerusalem, an envoy of Jews that included the high priest met him. Upon meeting the high priest, Alexander noticed the name of God engraved on the golden plate that covered the high priest's chest. After saluting the high priest, Alexander was greeted by the Jews. Although his companions' confusion by their leader's actions caused one to question him, an explanation revealed that Alexander had a dream from God that told of his conquering Persia (Josephus *Antiquities of the Jews* 11.8.5).

The high priest accompanied Alexander to Jerusalem where he offered a sacrifice and explained Daniel's prophecy concerning Alexander's conquest of Persia. The high priest's exposition of the prophecy led Alexander to favor the Jews to an extent that he asked what they would require of him. The high priest's request was that the Jews retain the traditions and religion of their fathers, and pay no tribute on the seventh year. Furthermore, the high priest made the same request for the exiles in Babylon and Media, and Alexander granted the requests. He also added that if any Jews desired to join his army, they would enjoy the same rights the priest had asked for. Many were prepared to accompany him in his wars. As this mighty warrior went about conquering, he eventually captured Persia. However, at the age of thirty-two he died, but those who would carry on his kingdom would divide it and continue to spread Hellenism.

THE SPREAD OF HELLENISM TO THE JEWS

When Alexander the Great died, his empire was divided among his generals. The Seleucids were the power that grew to have dominion over Jerusalem, and before their rule, the Ptolemies enjoyed control of Palestine. Both of these kingdoms were so named after Alexander's generals. Ptolemy I brought many Jews to Egypt and eventually witnessed the translation of the Hebrew Bible into Greek, known as the Septuagint (LXX). Egypt became a major center for Jews while under Ptolemaic rule (cf. Acts 2:10; 18:24).

Peace ended under the Ptolemaic rule when Antiochus III attempted to obtain Palestine from Egypt. Following a few failed attempts, the Seleucids captured Palestine from the grasp of the Ptolemies. During the Seleucid rule, a man named Jason bought the high priesthood. He promised a great tribute if the king would permit the building of a "place for exercise, and for the training up of youth in the fashions of the heathen, and to write them of Jerusalem by the name Antiochus" (2 Maccabees 4:9). Jason accelerated the nation into idolatry through compromise and by his greed for power. Jerusalem became a Greek city-state. The young men wore Greek hats, and the priests neglected their temple duties to exercise nakedly after the Grecian way; however, the worst was the procedure undergone by some Jews to reverse their circumcision.

In those days certain renegades came out from Israel and misled many, saying, "Let us go and make a covenant with the Gentiles around us, for since we separated from them many disasters have come upon us." This proposal pleased them, and some of the people eagerly went to the king, who authorized them to observe the ordinances of the Gentiles. So they built a gymnasium in Jerusalem, according to Gentile custom, and removed the marks of circumcision, and abandoned the holy covenant. They joined with the Gentiles and sold themselves to do evil. (1 Maccabees 1:11–15)

Undermined by another who sought his power, Jason lost the high priesthood to a higher bidder. Those who refused to compromise finally grew weary of Hellenization. A clear distinction became evident between the Hellenizers and the faithful. Those who sought to observe their covenant with God were known as the "pious." They aligned with the Maccabees and revolted in a holy war against the Seleucids that proved to be a turning point known as the Maccabean revolt.

THE LESSONS

Empires come and go, but the one thing that remains the same is our faith. Presidents come and go, but Christ remains. With the changes of empires and governing leaders, cultures sometimes change. Just look at how much the landscape of the United States changed under the Reagan or Obama administrations. Yet, the ancient message of holiness and righteousness stays the same and remains unaltered and unalterable. Therefore, put your faith in God, because governments and societies will change.

When culture comes knocking on your door as it did for the Jews, we can either fit in or stand apart. God, I believe, would have us stand apart from the nations and their ways and pursue His holiness.

According to the doings of the land of Egypt, where you dwelt, you shall not do; and according to the doings of the land of Canaan, where I am bringing you, you shall not do; nor shall you walk in their ordinances. 4 You shall observe My judgments and keep My ordinances, to walk in them: I am the Lord your God. (Leviticus 18:3–4)

This was, after all, what He wanted from Israel of old, so let us take this lesson with us today. Let's not be Americans, but citizens of heaven (Philippians 3:20).

FILL IN THE BLANK

1. King Ahasuerus was known to the Greeks as _____.

2. Ahasuerus attempted to conquer the Greeks and fought the _____ at the battle of Thermopylae.

3. Philip of _____ unified the _____.

4. Philip's son was _____ who spread Hellenism as he conquered.

5. _____ was the high priest of Israel who sold out the nation and allowed Hellenism in the country.

DISCUSSION QUESTIONS

1. Philip united Greece after the Persian invasions using fear from past events. Are modern politicians guilty of doing something similar? If so, how?

2. Since Alexander respected the Jewish religion, is it possible for us to respect other religions without necessarily buying into them? How about attending denominational worship services?

3. What are some things we do or ways we think as Americans that might be contradictory to our Christianity?

4. Does it help our biblical understanding to know what events were taking place in other places of the world at the same time. Why or why not?

5. Discuss the impact God's people had on other nations that conquered them. How did the faithful show these nations the power of God?

3

THE RISE OF JEWISH SECTS

Problems will arise with all people. When faced with those problems, groups are born in response to either support the action or object to it. We see this played out rather well in Western Christendom. The Roman Catholic Church began doing things that were suspect, so several led a Reformation that has since seen a plethora of splinters from the Roman Catholic Church, and since then there have been divisions even among their own denominations. Sadly, among even churches of Christ, there are differences in congregations—sound, liberal, progressive, feminist, anti-, and so on. The same can be seen in Intertestamental Judaism. Problems existed, so groups arose to counter those problems in their own ways. Therefore, in the New Testament, we see names like Pharisees and Sadducees when we fail to see them in the Old Testament. It will help our understanding of the Bible to understand the origins of these Jewish groups that were prominent during the time of Jesus.

FROM "PIOUS" TO "SEPARATED"

In the last lesson, I mentioned a group known as the "pious" who stood for the ancestral religious traditions of Israel. The "pious" later became Pharisees—a name meaning "separate." The "pious" who retired to the desert became the Essenes. The Pharisees were representatives of the Law— both oral and written. While the New Testament somewhat vilifies the Pharisees, their intentions were born of a concern for the preservation of Jewish culture, ceremonial purity (Mark 7:7ff), and protecting fellow Jews from transgressing God's commands (Matthew 12:1–2).

However, as is seen in Mark 12:13, they would align with dissenting groups when it was to their advantage. The Herodians mentioned there were pro-Rome while the Pharisees were not. The Pharisees wanted to preserve the purest sense of their religion and culture, so they generally despised the Herodians. However, in that scene, they hated Jesus more so. They occupied "Moses' seat" (Matthew 23:2)—a position of authority despite their hypocrisy—so they had plenty of influence within Judea, and they were able to turn the tides of public opinion with their adherence to the rabbinical oral law.

After Jason had lost the high priesthood to the higher bidder, Antiochus IV plundered the Temple to fund his conspiracy against Egypt. The higher bidder, Menelaus, and the Hellenizers modified the Temple worship so that Zeus earned honor instead of God. Antiochus ordered the Scriptures to be destroyed and all observances of Jewish religion forbidden. When the government expanded its laws to the rural areas, a priest named Mattathias refused to sacrifice to pagan gods. Mattathias refused to compromise his priesthood and killed a fellow Jew. Mattathias and his sons fled, and those who aligned with him rose up to engage in the Maccabean revolt.

Mattathias' son, Judas (his family name was "Hasmoneans,"

hence the Hasmonean Dynasty), picked up the torch in leading their guerilla war. Since the governing authorities pursued them into terrain more familiar to the Maccabees—a name meaning "hammer"—Judas and his followers enjoyed the advantage. Every effort to defeat the Maccabees met resistance that was impregnable. Due to other conflicts within the empire, the need for more troops was not entertained. Antiochus eventually withdrew the ban on Judaism; however, the high-priesthood remained with Menelaus. A new altar adorned the refurbished Temple, in addition to sacred furniture, and a new festival occupied the Jewish calendar as a celebration of this victory—Hanukkah. With the political threat somewhat isolated, Judas turned his attention to the religious threat of Hellenization. Menelaus was deposed and a new high priest installed. The "pious" withdrew from the revolt when the new high priest formally recognized that they were the orthodox adherents to and advocates of the Law. Judas continued with his revolt until he was killed in battle in 160 B.C.

Judas' brothers, Jonathan and Simon, would follow his rule, but assassins would end their lives. John Hyrcanus, Simon's son, rose to the high priesthood secured by his uncle, Jonathan. Becoming the high priest meant that Jonathan had previously accepted it from someone who based his right to bestow it on a claim to be the son of Antiochus. Before Jonathan became high priest, history is unclear as to who held the office. Suggestions answering this question do not fully harmonize. However, with John Hyrcanus as the new high priest, the Pharisees emerged to oppose the Hasmoneans serving a dual role as high priest and ethnarch; however, the Sadducees supported Hyrcanus (*Antiquities of the Jews* 13.10.5–6).

DESERT DWELLERS

The Essenes—a group we don't read about in the New Testament—were a segment of the "pious" that retired to the desert after the Maccabean revolt. They were like a monastic group whose rules on personal purity through the observation of lustrations, or cleansings, were stringent. They refused to participate in the Temple sacrifices because they felt the Temple had been polluted by the corrupt priesthood. Instead, they would send their dedication to the Temple, but would offer no living sacrifice (*Antiquities of the Jews* 18.1.5; Philo *Quod Omn. Prob.* 12.75). The depiction of this group by Philo (ca. 25 B.C. —A.D. 50) is what modern readers would identify as monks. This isolationist group cultivated the ground and was a poor, free, and highly moral people opposed to war. (*Quod Omn. Prob.* 12.76-79). Because of these attributes, they were unlike the other sects. However, they were like the Pharisees in that they were students and adherents of the Mosaic Law.

THE ARISTOCRATS

While their origin is ambiguous, the Sadducees were aristocrats. They were typically priests, and they differed with the Pharisees by enjoying the favor of the rich while the Pharisees enjoyed the confidence of the populace (*Antiquities of the Jews* 13.10.6; cf. 18.1.4). The Sadducees were not strangers to conflict with the Pharisees, although, they would side with the Pharisees from time-to-time to be tolerated by the populace (*Antiquities of the Jews* 18.1.4). They argued against the oral law and advocated that the Law was higher than the prophets (cf. Matthew 22:23–33). They did not believe in the resurrection, angels, or the spirit (Acts 23:6–9; Mark 12:18; cf. *Antiquities of the Jews* 18.1.4), and furthermore, they denied the Greek notion of fate altogether (*Antiquities of the Jews* 13.5.9). They also believed a particular contribution should be made for sacrifices and that sacrifices should not be funded by the Temple treasury. As witnessed by their support of the Hasmoneans, they were undoubtedly supporters of

Rome. Because of this support, they enjoyed primary influence within the Sanhedrin—a governing body of twenty-three to seventy-one religious and political leaders for the Jews. Their political ideology gave them willingness to compromise, which led to the adoption of Hellenistic tendencies.

MAINTAINING JUDAISM

Through a broken succession of rule, the Hasmoneans eventually were faced with a civil war when two brothers—sons of Hyrcanus—battled over who was to be king. After John Hyrcanus' son died, his daughter-in-law, Salome Alexander, married John's other son, who was designated high priest and king by Salome. He also died, but he bequeathed the kingdom to her to rule. Under Salome's rule, the Pharisees would rise as the majority both politically and religiously. Salome "restored again those practices which the Pharisees had introduced, according to the traditions of their forefathers.... [T]he Pharisees had the authority" (*Antiquities of the Jews* 13.16.2).

Salome made her son, Hyrcanus, the high priest. Although the Pharisees held disdain for the Hasmoneans as priests, they permitted Hyrcanus to serve because he had a reserved demeanor. The Pharisees were able to do what they wanted without interference from the queen or high priest. Salome went as far as commanding the people to obey the Pharisees. After their mother died, Hyrcanus lost his position to his brother, Aristobulus. The Idumean governor, Antipater, rallied behind Hyrcanus whose disposition allowed him to accept the defeat. As Antipater always remained in favor with the ruling power of Rome, he eventually would gain the ultimate approval by aiding Caesar's invasion of Egypt. For this act, Antipater became procurator of Judea and obtained Roman citizenship. After Antipater was poisoned, his son, Herod, became king of the Jews by the authority of Mark Antony—a contemporary of Julius Caesar. This Herod was king when Jesus was born, and his sons maintained the throne throughout the New Testament. With this new rule, and since Aristobulus' usurpation of the high priesthood, the Pharisees' political power faded, so they turned their concentration on influencing the nation to a local level through the synagogue.

THE LESSONS

I want to point out that while these groups were not necessarily "biblical" in the sense that we can read about them in the Old Testament, they were never preached against by Christ for their existence. Sure, Jesus had a lot to say against the Pharisees—their hypocrisy and the like—but Christ also urged the Jews, "Therefore whatever they tell you to observe, that observe and do, but do not do according to their works; for they say, and do not do" (Matthew 23:3). Jesus realized that they were good teachers, but they were poor doers. What they taught was rather favorable in Christ's eyes as long as it adhered to Moses' Law, but they were not to be followed for their example.

Sometimes we in churches of Christ are rather quick to dismiss what anyone says if they belong to a denomination or if their church has a name other than "Church of Christ." Please hear me out—I'm a preacher and believer in being simply what the disciples were in the New Testament. Yet, just because someone bears an unbiblical name doesn't mean that they're wrong 100% of the time. Even a broken clock is right twice a day. Jesus recognized the Pharisees' capacity for teaching sound doctrine as it were, even if their example was horrible.

There are many denominational teachers, preachers, and scholars who give an excellent teaching on many aspects of God's Word. However, the things they do poorly are usually crucial matters. We can hear them out and even follow what they say as long as it's good Bible teaching, but if they err in points of doctrine we should always follow God's Word. I could list the denominational people whose works I love reading, and I have many friends who share my sentiments. Perhaps one of my favorite authors ever is C. S. Lewis, and he was Anglican. I wouldn't necessarily agree with him if he told me how to be saved, but I can use good judgment and pick up the wisdom he may provide here or there.

FILL IN THE BLANK

1. The group known as the "_____" later became the _____.

2. The group that retired to the desert were called the _____.

3. The Sadducees didn't believe in _____, _____, and _____.

4. The Maccabees' family name was _____.

5. Once the Pharisees lost political power, they directed their attention to the _____.

DISCUSSION QUESTIONS

1. The Pharisees prove that when a person loses political power, they can still have a tremendous influence through local means. Why do so many put their hopes on political power rather than through some medium of local impact, and how might you use the local influence of the church for good?

2. What might we suggest by Jesus not denouncing the Pharisees or Sadducees because they're not mentioned in the Bible? How would this, if at all, apply to our modern views on denominationalism?

3. Since each of these sects grew out of a reaction to something, how might we be more proactive (vs. reactive) to avoid some of the troubles that arise within the church or our own lives?

4. What can we learn from the flaws of the Pharisees as we look at both their teaching and their examples? In what ways might we bring forth a scriptural teaching that is not followed with an example that would be Christ-like? How can we take measures to identify and avoid these things?

5. How does learning of the origins of the Sadducees and Pharisees, and even the Essenes, help in your understanding of the Bible? Is it helpful to understand the origins of different religious groups today?

4

THE RISE OF THE SYNAGOGUE

One institution that we read of in the New Testament but is mainly absent from the Old Testament is the synagogue. The term "synagogue" derives from Greek and means "we go together" or "assembly." In the first century, the synagogue was the heart of Judaism, and we read where Jesus attended synagogue services. The Pharisees taught in synagogues, and from here we may also see it not as a religious center but also as an ancient community center of some sort. However, in the backdrop of the synagogue was the primary place of worship—the Temple.

THE TEMPLE

While the synagogue played a significant role in the lives of the Jews during New Testament times, it was not intended to replace the Temple. Rather, the purpose of the synagogue was supplementary to Temple worship. The Temple had been rebuilt when the Jews returned to Jerusalem from captivity (Ezra, Nehemiah). The period of time from when the Temple was rebuilt in the late sixth century B.C.

until it was destroyed by the Romans in A.D. 70 is known as "Second Temple Judaism." This period consists of foreign occupation and the rule of Palestine—first by the Persians (538–332 B.C.), second by the Greeks (332–63 B.C.), and finally by the Romans (63 B.C.–A.D. 70).

Herod remodeled the Temple to expand its beauty and grandeur. He appears to have done this only after spending considerable sums of money building lavish temples and cities to honor his Roman lord (*Antiquities of the Jews* 15.9.5; 15.11.3). During the first century, the Temple was frequented daily for prayer and worship (Matthew 26:55; Luke 2:37; 24:53; Acts 2:46; 3:1). Even the earliest Christians who were Jewish continued meeting at the Temple in Christianity's early decades.

These two institutions—the synagogue and Temple—were vital to Judaism. The Temple represented God's presence among His people, while the synagogue was a comfort from the corrupt aristocratic priesthood. Both served as a precursor to the church and New Covenant whereby Christ would save and establish His church (cf. Matthew 16:18).

THE HOUSE OF PRAYER

Because of the deportation from the Promised Land after the destruction of the Temple by the Babylonians, faithful Jews sought to maintain their heritage through an observance of the moral precepts of the law. The origin of the synagogue is widely debated. Some believe that the synagogue was always a part of Jewish life (cf. Ezekiel 11:16; 14:1), but others pinpoint its origins to the exilic or post-exilic period.

Before the Jewish deportation to Babylon in 586 B.C., the ceremony of the Temple reigned supreme within the life of Jewish religion for those who were faithful. The deficiency that led to the Jewish captivity was the lack of moral living and idolatry in spite of ceremonial observation as is attested to by the prophets (Jeremiah 7:21–23; Amos 5:21–24; Micah 6:6–8; cf. John 4:24). With their removal from their land and the destruction of the Temple, the people dedicated themselves to learning God's precepts and applying them to their lives. We see hints of this with Ezra the scribe (Ezra 7:10). The synagogue served as the means to this end.

Philo described the synagogue as a house of prayer—a place where Jewish national customs were preserved and social privileges were exercised. Philo noted that the synagogues were also free of empirical statues for three hundred years until Caligula's reign which began in 37 A.D. (*Flacc.* 7.47–8.53; *Leg.* 20.138; cf. *Antiquities of the Jews* 18.8.4; 19.6.3). However, before Caligula's reign, Caesar Augustus (27 B.C. –A.D. 14) placed the synagogue under a blanket of protection. Augustus swore that anyone who stole the "holy books, or their sacred money" would have his possessions seized and placed in the Roman treasury (*Antiquities of the Jews* 16.6.2).

A synagogue meeting could not convene unless ten males were present. The worship of the synagogue began with benedictions, which preceded the Shema ("Hear") from Deuteronomy 6:4. At least eighteen eulogies were offered during the time of Christ; however, nineteen exist now. The reader of the Shema would also recite these prayers, and afterward, he would read from the scrolls of the Law and prophets. After reading a selection from the prophets, the presider would preach a homily, or sermon, with which the service concluded.

A PRECURSOR TO THE CHURCH

Spring-boarding from the synagogue meeting, students of history will notice that the synagogue had many similarities to church worship meetings.

The prevailing theory of the early history of the Christian liturgy [worship] is that the Christian order of worship was built up from the Jewish synagogue service of scripture teaching and prayer with the addition of the distinctively Christian rite of the Lord's supper….The synagogue service included Scripture readings, interspersed with Psalm chants, a sermon, prayers, and almsgiving.[1]

When Paul and Silas were in the Philippian jail in Acts 16:25, they were singing a prayer to God. While the majority of the English versions render this verse "singing and praying," the original Greek indicates that they might have been singing or chanting a Psalm. A distinction in modern worship assemblies is the execution of praise. However, prayers, sermons, offerings, and Scripture readings remain similar in most Christian assemblies. The Lord's Supper was the unique distinction between the synagogue service and the church's worship meeting.

By the time of Christ, the synagogue was the most important place when compared to the Temple. From the Bible, one observes several similarities between the church and the synagogue.

Practice	Synagogue	Church
Scripture Reading	Luke 4:16; Acts 13:5	Acts 17:11; 1 Timothy 4:13
Preaching/Teaching	Matthew 13:54; Mark 1:21; Acts 13:15, 42	1 Corinthians 14:3; 1 Timothy 4:13
Withdrawal of Fellowship	John 9:22; 12:42	1 Corinthians 5
Discipline	Acts 22:19; 26:11	Matthew 18:15–17; 1 Corinthians 5; 2 Thessalonians 3

While this table represents only a few similarities from Scripture, other sources show that singing was a part of the synagogue meetings as well as almsgiving. The officers of the synagogue correspond somewhat to the prescribed officers of the church. The synagogue had a chief ruler which was somewhat comparable to the duties of a minister of the church (Acts 18:8, 17; cf. Ephesians 4:11; 2 Timothy 4:2–5). Also, there were rulers of the synagogue which parallel the elders/bishops (Mark 5:22, 35; 8:41; cf. Acts 14:23; Philippians 1:1; 1 Timothy 3:1ff; Titus 1:5; 1 Peter 5:1). To neglect the comparisons of the church to the synagogue would almost strip the church of its heritage.

When the first batch of Christians became Christian, they continued doing what they had always done. In its early decades, Christianity wasn't seen as much a distinct religion as it was seen as another branch of Judaism. With the spread of Christianity to the Gentiles and the uttermost parts of the world, it then began to take on a unique status as its own religion. However, Christianity is a religion rooted in Judaism that is as ancient as one might hope for it to be.

THE LESSONS

Though not scripturally mandated, the synagogue was certainly no hindrance to fidelity. As a matter of fact, it was an aid in the same way that Sunday school or Bible study is an aid for the Christian. When a person has enough discernment, they learn to see how things and practices become conducive to our growth in faith while also recognizing what may be additions or innovations to God's Word. The synagogue was one such aid to Jewish fidelity to the Law.

Another lesson from this is that though the leadership of the Temple, the Sadducees, were corrupt, it didn't mean that the Temple itself or God's design for the Temple was corrupt. In our day, many congregations are going down paths that they see as progress. They will usually begin by announcing a new practice by stating something like, "After much study and prayer, we the elders have decided…" Sometimes these decisions of "progress" are actual progress, while at other times they may be decisions of departure from Scripture.

There are also some Christians who can see nothing but broken-ness in the church, so they make it their personal mission to be the advocates of a movement to make the church better. You and I can-not make the church better because it is by being the Bride of Christ what God intends it to be. If there's anything wrong with the church, it's the people in it. Even still, if our views of the church are that she must be a perfect institution, we miss the point of Romans 5:8, "But God demonstrates His own love toward us, in that while we were still sinners, Christ died for us." Human nature is flawed, even when it professes Christ as Lord. Yet, that doesn't mean that the church is bad because she has been designed by God for sanctification to glo-rify Him. A fellow preacher has a saying, "If you ever find the perfect church, don't join it because you'll ruin it." We must realize that the church is a place where grace resides. Because grace lives within the Bride of Christ, the need to show grace exists. Introducing instru-ments won't make her better, because to Christ she's already perfect despite her flaws. Making women preachers won't do anything to enhance her beauty because there is no distinction within her.

The Jews continued to worship at the Temple, the place where God wanted them to worship, and they worshipped in the way God wanted them to worship. Although the priests and high-priests were corrupt, the design of worship was not the problem. The problems existed because men chose not to follow the directions God set forth. Even when God's people were not being faithful to him, the Temple stood in the distance in Palestine as a reminder of God. We should put forth every effort to let the church be seen as a reminder of Christ's grace where reformed sinners are gathering to be the righteousness of God through Christ Jesus.

One final lesson can be this—study the first-century synagogue if you want to better understand the first-century church. The similarities in their exercises during meetings and their organizations remove a bunch of the denominational baggage that churches try to adopt. As 21st century Christians, we read the Bible with a particular intellectual strain. Therefore, we forget that the ancient church was modeled after the synagogue, and therefore did things a certain way. If we better understood this, then perhaps we wouldn't waste time over whether or not to form a group and call them a praise team to make our singing sound better or other such ideas meant to change our worship. The simplicity of first-century meetings in the church derived from the synagogue, and that same simplicity ought to be enough for us in the 21st century.

FILL IN THE BLANK

1. The word "synagogue" means _____
   _____.

2. The period of time from the rebuilding of the Temple under the Persians until it was destroyed by the Romans was known as _____.

3. Philo described the synagogue as a _____.

4. A synagogue could not convene unless _____ males were present.

5. The _____ was the unique distinction between the synagogue service and the church's worship meeting.

DISCUSSION QUESTIONS

1. Discuss the point at which something is either an aid or an addition to God's Word. Think about song books, Power-Point, and then reflect on instrumental worship.

2. How should we respond when we become disenchanted with the church? What is at work within our dissatisfaction?

3. Do the innovations and additions to religious practice suggest an ignorance not only of God's Word but also of history?

4. How does understanding the role of the synagogue to the Jews help us as Christians to better understand the church?

5. When did the Christian religion begin to be viewed as distinct from Judaism? What do we need to focus on to remain distinct from other religions?

NOTES

1. Everett Ferguson, *Early Christians Speak: Faith and Life in the First Three Centuries*, 3d. ed. (Abilene Christian University Press, 1999), 84.

5

GETTING BACK IN GOD'S WORD

The previous two lessons centered on the Jewish response to the spread of Hellenism. When the Hellenist culture reached Palestine, the Maccabean revolt was the answer. That revolt birthed religious sects and gave a focus to local teaching in the synagogue. However, it would be a large oversight to neglect that the birth of these sects and the center of synagogue learning had as their undergirding a dedication to the study of the Law.

THE PLACE OF SCRIPTURE IN THE OLD TESTAMENT

When Joshua's generation died, the nation, because of its neglect of hearing the law (cf. Deuteronomy 31:10–13), was thrust into a repetitive cycle in the book of Judges. The cycle that followed was: Israel's infidelity, God's removal of divine protection, foreign oppression, Israel's cry to God, God raising a judge to deliver Israel, and the cycle would repeat with Israel's infidelity. Throughout Judges, the deliverers would often be reminded of the basic history of Israel as a nation when God delivered them—something that would not have gone without notice and appreciation had the Law been read as the Law prescribed.

When Israel demanded a monarch for the purpose of being like other nations, one of the monarchical commandments given was that the king was to have a written deposit of the law for private study (Deuteronomy 17:18–20; cf. Psalm 1). It was the duty of the priests to whom Moses had entrusted the safekeeping of the law to grant this written deposit (Deuteronomy 31:9, 25–26). Not only would the monarch have a responsibility to personally study the law—which is often reflected in the Davidic psalms—but the Levitical order had a duty to ensure that the king had a written deposit for such use.

It is unclear if the Levitical order procured and dispensed a copy of the Torah for Saul the Benjamite because Saul's reign could be characterized as a rebellion not only to the words of the prophet and judge Samuel but also to God. Samuel wrote a book about the rights and duties of the kingship that was laid before God (1 Samuel 10:25; cf. 8:11–18), but it is unknown whether or not Saul consulted that book. There is no mention of "the Law" or "the Law of Moses" in all of 1 Samuel.

It is clear that the Law was consulted in David's reign, but it is not recorded that the seventh-year reading took place from the time of Joshua until Josiah was king of Judah. When David transported the Ark from the house of Abinadab to Jerusalem, the scene that unfolded was an unauthorized carriage of the Ark that resulted in the death of Uzzah when he sought to steady the Ark when it was disturbed. Later, when it appeared that David consulted the Law (1 Chronicles 15:1–13), the Ark was transported according to the Mosaic mandate concerning its relocation and handling.

The next public reading came after the high priest Hilkiah found the book of the Law in the Temple during the reign of King Josiah of Judah. Hilkiah took the book to the king's secretary who then took it to the king. Upon hearing the words of the book of the Law, King Josiah grieved and sent to inquire of the Lord because all the curses of the book were to be rendered to the wicked people of Judah (2 Kings 22–23; 2 Chronicles 34).

When Josiah assembled the people to have the book of the law read in their hearing, Josiah led a covenant renewal to which the people consented. However, after so many years of apostasy that began with King Solomon, changing the trajectory of Judah was unrealized because of so many years of neglecting to read the law. Therefore, the land was purged of its inhabitants so that it could undergo a period of cleansing (cf. Leviticus 18:28; 20:22).

The prophetic era in Israel's divided history served the function of a public oration rather than reading. Isaiah and Jeremiah commanded that the book of the Lord be read to consult the prophecies revealed to them by God (Isaiah 34:16; cf. 30:8; Jeremiah 36:6ff). During this time, the prophetic corpus of writings seemed to have been born and added to the Torah of Israel as a part of their canon. The failure to adhere to the legal and prophetic warnings led to the eventual exile of the northern kingdom under the Assyrians and, later, the southern kingdom by the Babylonians.

When those of the exile were permitted to return to their land after decades of absence, they did so. Sometime later, Ezra arrived to lead them. Ezra was described as one who "set his heart to study the Law of the LORD, and to do it and to teach his statutes and rules in Israel" (Ezra 7:10). Ezra's knowledge of the Law enabled him to be the advocate for the Law in the reestablishment of Israel, so when the people were assembled for a reading of the Law, their response was remorse and weeping (Nehemiah 8:9). Their response to the public reading unveiled that their ancestors had long neglected the attention the Law warranted. Because of this neglect, their exile was explained and understood.

The return from exile and covenant renewal did not prohibit a lukewarm response to the Law in the future. By the time of the prophet Malachi, the priests had turned from the Law (Malachi 4:4). Their neglect of the Law, perhaps a response to unfulfilled eschatological expectations given by the prophets, led them to apathy towards religious observance. Neglecting their duties manifested in the lack of reverence towards God, and instead of teaching the law, they turned from it (Malachi 2:1–9).

Throughout the history of Israel as a nation, their political journey with God began with a reading that was heard by a subsequent generation, but from the time of Joshua until Josiah it was scarce if not non-existent. When they were finally exiled, reading and hearing the law would be the cornerstone of restoration for Israel. As long as they heeded the Torah and gave attention to its reading, God's people seemed to remain faithful to him. Whenever the reading and hearing were neglected, the people were destroyed for a lack and rejection of knowledge. The cultural battle that Israel faced when Hellenism spread to Jerusalem is another national challenge that would serve as an impetus to their adherence to the law.

A REVOLUTION FOR THE LAW BETWEEN THE TESTAMENTS

Throughout the Intertestamental Period, the public reading was given attention. The practice is assumed to have been taking place by the time of the Maccabean revolt when the books of the Law were seized from the Temple and from any who possessed copies. The seizure was followed by a subsequent destruction of the copies of the law, which gave a rise to Jewish zeal for the customs of their ancestors (1 Maccabees 1:56–57).

Mattathias Maccabee, in rejection of foreign occupation and decree, vowed not to desert the Law and called for all who were zealous for the Law to stand with him in rebellion against the foreign rule (1 Maccabees 2:21, 27). When Jerusalem was overtaken by foreign occupants, the Jews fasted in sackcloth and searched the book of the Law concerning why Gentiles occupied the land. After that, the Maccabees determined to restore to observance through a study of the Law what had been lost, but because the Temple was no longer in the hands of the Jews, they determined to fight the Gentiles. If God would see them to victory, they believed it would be to His glory; but if God did not see them to victory, it was His will (1 Maccabees 3:48–60). Later in the story of the Maccabees, the law again surfaced in a public reading when Eleazar was appointed to be the reader before going into battle (2 Maccabees 8:23; cf. 1 Maccabees 3:48).

During foreign oppression, the Jews relied heavily upon the Law, whereas it was ignored previously in their history during the Old Testament. They clung to their religion during these and subsequent times (3 Maccabees 1:12).

> In the time of my maturity I remained with my husband, and when these sons had grown up their father died. A happy man was he, who lived out his life with good children, and did not have the grief of bereavement. While he was still with you, he taught you the law and the prophets. He read to you about Abel slain by Cain, and Isaac who was offered as a burnt offering, and about Joseph in prison. (4 Maccabees 18:9–11)

> Baruch read the words of this book to Jeconiah son of Jehoiakim, king of Judah, and to all the people who came to hear the book.... And you shall read aloud this scroll that we are sending you, to make your confession in the house of the Lord on the days of the festivals and at appointed seasons. (Baruch 1:3, 14; cf. Tobit 12:12; 1 Maccabees 5:14)

There were no judges appointed or prophets sent (Josephus *Against Apion* 1.8), but only a strict adherence to the Law that began with Ezra and Nehemiah. By this time, the practice of Law observance was ingrained in the hearts of those who wanted to avoid another exile because the Jews learned that it was their neglect of the Law through public readings that led to their oppression and displacement from the land.

THE LESSONS

One of the major concerns of the Essenes was preserving God's commands, and they actually believed that their interpretation was the final interpretation of the Law. They felt that their study of the Law atoned for the land. Philo mentioned a monastic sect called, "Therapeutae" who read Scripture and gave homilies on Scripture at their banquets (*Vit. Cont.* 9–10). The tide of religious practice had turned. The Law was finally being given the attention it deserved. However, that would not be without problems. Rival interpretations would arise as we see even in our own day, but at least, we can say that they were in God's Word—no matter how misguided some might have been. The lesson here is that it is important to be in God's Word, and it's also important to be in God's Word to understand it correctly. Never forsake, as the Jews once had, the life-giving instructions in favor of what we may think is better, because God is always the best choice.

FILL IN THE BLANK

1. In the Old Testament, the Law was to be read every _____ years.

2. From the time of Joshua until _____, there is no mention of the Law being read.

3. The priest _____ found the Book of the Law in the Temple and had it read to King Josiah.

4. _____ the scribe set his heart to know God's Law and teach it in Israel.

5. By the time of the prophet _____ the priests had turned from the Law.

DISCUSSION QUESTIONS

1. Considering the path Israel went down when the Law was ignored, how might that correlate to the United States as the Bible's influence has been diminished?

2. Since people of old didn't typically have several copies of the Bible as we have, why are we so biblically illiterate while they were more pious?

3. The lesson is clear that a knowledge of God's Word results in fidelity and God's favor. Will the church and her members not learn from history the importance of placing God's Word at the front of their lives even if it means fewer sports, hunting, fishing, golfing, shopping, etc.? What are some ways we can make sure our priorities are in the right places?

4. What are some practical ways you have found to help yourself or your family be a better Bible student?

5. In reading about the Israelites during the time of the Judges, we can observe the repetitive cycle of Israel's infidelity, God's removal of divine protection, foreign oppression, Israel's cry to God, God raising a judge to deliver Israel, and then the

cycle would repeat with Israel's infidelity. Are there times where our own spiritual lives tend to fall into a repetitive cycle? How would that cycle be like or different from the Israelites? How can we break the cycle?

6

THE CANONIZATION OF THE OLD TESTAMENT

Since the Jews began giving more and more attention to the Law, it would only be reasonable that their fidelity to the study of God's Word, coupled with foreign invasion, would spur them to collect their sacred writings into a canon. The term "canon" itself is a Greek term that means "measuring reed." It's used to denote a standard, and in this case, the standard was the inspired, God-breathed sacred texts of Judaism.

THE TRIPARTITE DIVISION

By the time of the prophets, the canon of the Old Testament—to the Hebrews called the "Tanakh"—consisted of three divisions of literature: the law, the prophets, and the writings.

> Then they said, "Come and let us devise plans against Jeremiah; for the law shall not perish from the priest,

nor counsel from the wise, nor the word from the prophet." (Jeremiah 18:18; 586–570 B.C.)

The priest's instructions pertained to the law, the words of the wise made up the writings, and the prophets delivered messages to God's people about their current circumstances and looked forward to the hope that God offered.

The same division is witnessed in the Intertestamental Period too. The prologue to Ecclesiasticus (ca. 200–175 B.C.)—which was also known as the Wisdom of Sirach, Sirach, or Ben Sira, and not to be confused with Ecclesiastes—identified "the law, and the prophets, and other books of our fathers"; "the law...the prophets, and the rest of the books." Even later we see a similar division.

> The same things are reported in the records and in the memoirs of Nehemiah, and also that he founded a library and collected the books about the kings and prophets, and the writings of David, and letters of kings about votive offerings. In the same way Judas also collected all the books that had been lost on account of the war that had come upon us, and they are in our possession. (2 Maccabees 2:13–14; 124 B.C.)

The notion of a canon actually began to arise during this period when Judea was under attack. Nehemiah had collected a body of books, but war threatened them. Often in wars, people would demolish monuments and libraries to erase a people's history, so preserving the literary works of Israel became a concern because of war, as well as to preserve Jewish culture and religious fidelity. Philo (25 B.C.–50 A.D.) gives us another insight into the Old Testament.

And in every house there is a sacred shrine which is called the holy place, and the monastery in which they retire by themselves and perform all the mysteries of a holy life, bringing in nothing, neither meat, nor drink, nor anything else which is indispensable towards supplying the necessities of the body, but studying in that place the laws and the sacred oracles of God enunciated by the holy prophets, and hymns, and psalms, and all kinds of other things by reason of which knowledge and piety are increased and brought to perfection. (*On the Contemplative Life* 3.25)

Not only did he mention the prophets, but he added the hymns and psalms. The point of these works, he wrote, was to increase in knowledge and piety.

When Luke wrote his gospel account in A.D. 60–61, he also recognized this tripartite division: "Then He said to them, 'These are the words which I spoke to you while I was still with you, that all things must be fulfilled which were written in the Law of Moses and the Prophets and the Psalms concerning Me.' And He opened their understanding, that they might comprehend the Scriptures" (Luke 24:44–45). Jesus recognized the body of books esteemed by the Jews just as Jeremiah had. However, exactly how the books should have been classified is a matter of discussion because Jesus referred to the Psalms as Law on one occasion (John 10:34).

THE NUMBER OF BOOKS

As to the number of books in the Old Testament, Josephus (A.D. 37–100) wrote that there were only twenty-two books the Hebrews esteemed as Scripture (*Against Apion* 1.8). The book of 2 Esdras, an apocalyptic work, identified twenty-four books of the Tanakh at the time between the destruction of Jerusalem by the Romans in A.D. 70 and A.D. 100.

> So during the forty days, ninety-four books were written. And when the forty days were ended, the Most High spoke to me, saying, "Make public the twenty-four books that you wrote first, and let the worthy and the unworthy read them; but keep the seventy that were written last, in order to give them to the wise among your people. For in them is the spring of understanding, the fountain of wisdom, and the river of knowledge." And I did so. (2 Esdras 14:44–48)

The reason for a distinction in number may have to do with the fact that sometimes books were included as a part of another. For example, some considered Jeremiah and Lamentations as one book, while Ruth and Judges were one book. Second Esdras may have separated one of more of these to make the number twenty-four. What must also be remembered was that the Minor Prophets were all one book and not twelve individual books in canonical numbering. Both Origen (A.D. 185–251) and Jerome (A.D. 347–419)—early Christian theologians, the latter of whom received rabbinical training—numbered twenty-two books.

The earliest Christian list of the Old Testament came from Melito of Sardis and was compiled about A.D. 170.

> "Of Moses, five books: Genesis, Exodus, Numbers, Leviticus, Deuteronomy; Jesus Nave [Joshua], Judges, Ruth; of Kings, four books [1 and 2 Samuel; 1 and 2 Kings]; of Chronicles, two; the Psalms of David, the Proverbs of Solomon, Wisdom also [Apocrypha], Ecclesiastes, Song of Songs, Job; of Prophets, Isaiah,

Jeremiah; of the twelve prophets, one book [minor prophets]; Daniel, Ezekiel, Esdras [Ezra and Nehemiah]. From which also I have made the extracts, dividing them into six books." Such are the words of Melito (Eusebius Ecclesiastical History 4.26.14).

This list is rather close to the Old Testament that we have, yet it adds an apocryphal book and omits Esther.

WHEN THE CANON WAS SETTLED

When Jerusalem was destroyed by the Romans in A.D. 70, the Sanhedrin ("Council") could no longer meet in Jerusalem. For the Jews in the first century, this body of leaders was vital to national identity. One of their antecedents was the council of elders during the Intertestamental Period (1 Maccabees 12:6; 2 Maccabees 4:49; 11:27). In the New Testament, the chief priests, elders, and scribes composed the body.

Once destroyed, a group of rabbis made their way to the rabbinical school of Jamnia (Jabneh) to assume legislative authority over Judaism. Many believe that the council of Jamnia that met in A.D. 90 was the final deciding point of which books belonged in the Old Testament canon. Other sources attest that this was not the case since works under question at this council had already been used as Scripture. Regardless, whenever the books were decided is of no grave consequence since Melito of Sardis' list only slightly differs from the list we currently esteem.

Judaism was a rather bookish religion. In addition to the Old Testament, or Tanakh, the writings of the rabbis included the Talmud, Mishnah, and Gemara as well as other writings. Many Israelite writings no longer exist—such as "Book of the Wars of the Lord"

(Numbers 21:14); "Book of Jashar" (Joshua 10:13); and "Book of the Acts of Solomon" (1 Kings 11:41). The list that we have—which is referred to as the "Protestant Bible"—follows the same list of the Hebrew Bible while Catholic and Orthodox Bible's include more books in their Old Testaments.

THE LESSONS

Our 21st-century Western minds see the formation of the Bible differently than how the ancients might have perceived it. We are Biblicists—that is, we call Bible things by Bible names and search the Scripture for a "thus says the Lord" for everything we do. I'm not saying this is wrong, but I will say that it can be taken too far. Christians can pick micro-statements from passages and hang a doctrine upon that micro-statement. A meta-narrative is likely more necessary. Meta-narrative sees the big picture. We sometimes focus on the minuteness to the degree that we end up proof-texting.

Assuredly, Jesus regarded the jot and tittle of the Law, and so should we. However, His jot and tittle aren't necessarily ours. We must remember the purpose of the Old Testament as well as our New Testament. Jesus said of the Old, "You search the Scriptures, for in them you think you have eternal life; and these are they which testify of Me" (John 5:39). Should we see the value of God's Bible? Yes. But, we should never esteem the Bible without Christ, for it's the Bible that points us to faith in Him. The Pharisees and some of our brethren believe that a mastering of the text leads to eternal life when it's Christ who gives us eternal life. The Scriptures testify about Him and not exclusively a legalist list of do's and don'ts (cf. Luke 24:27, 45).

Another lesson that I might add is that I'd hope that we rightly esteem the Bible as the ancients did. I once attended a synagogue Sabbath service. I noticed that the rabbi didn't touch the actual scroll on which God's Words were. I later asked her—yes, it was a progressive synagogue who had a female rabbi—why she used a stylus to touch the scroll. She told me that it was for two reasons. The first was practical—the scroll of her synagogue was several hundred years old, so to touch it would hurt the material and cause it to decay quicker. Second, no rabbi touches the actual scroll with their bare hand except for special circumstances, because those are God's Words, and they wouldn't want to treat God with contempt because of their sinfulness. I found this explanation very compelling as to the Jews' reverence of the Torah.

Let this be a lesson for us. Even Muslims, so I'm told, won't allow any book to be placed higher than their Quran on a shelf. They won't take it to the bathroom or put it on the floor. If they have such reverence for heresy, shouldn't we have as much if not more for God's Holy Word much like the Jews? Furthermore, we shouldn't just plop our Bibles in the pew and leave them there as if the only time we use them is during worship. Sometimes familiarity breeds contempt, and our having multiple Bibles may sometimes spoil us and lead us to take for granted that the Bible is not just another good book one ought to read. Rather, it's God's Holy and Divine Word. It should be treated as such and esteemed as such in our hearts and minds.

FILL IN THE BLANK

1. The Hebrews called their Bible the _____.

2. The Bible was divided into three divisions, and they are _____, _____, and _____.

3. The earliest Christian list comes to us from _____ of _____ in the year A.D. _____.

4. Many believe that the Old Testament canon was settled at the Council of _____ in A.D. _____.

5. The council convened in order to replace the _____ that was disbanded with the destruction of Jerusalem.

DISCUSSION QUESTIONS

1. Is the canon open or closed? That is, can more books be added (open) or has the matter been settled (closed)? Discuss why.

2. With the differing lists and numbers of books that existed, how can we be sure that we have all the books that were divinely inspired?

3. When, if ever, might it become a bad thing to study the Bible too much?

4. What are some misleading doctrines that have been formed because of people using a "micro-statement" in a passage without considering the big picture?

5. "Sometimes familiarity breeds contempt, and our having multiple Bibles may sometimes spoil us and lead us to take for granted that the Bible is not just another good book one ought to read." Discuss this statement. Do you agree or disagree with it?

7

THE APOCRYPHA

The books that have been omitted from the Old Testament canon are one large point of contention. Differing traditions within Christendom include them while the churches of Christ particularly don't. Why is that? Several factors surround the inclusion or exclusion of these books. Many brethren try to make a case for renouncing them by looking at their content and denouncing their inspiration—something I wouldn't dismiss altogether. However, I think a better case can be made for excluding them by examining the history of these books.

It's rather clear from history whether they were or weren't included in the canon. Furthermore, their exclusion from the canon notwithstanding, it doesn't mean that they are "evil" books that should be avoided at all costs. After all, they were written for a purpose, so our studies will be the most profitable if these books are allowed to serve the same purpose to us that they served to the Jews of old.

OMITTED FROM THE JEWISH CANON

The Apocrypha (meaning "hidden") is a group of writings that date from 300 B.C. to A.D. 100. They consist of historical writings (1 Esdras, 1 & 2 Maccabees), fiction (Tobit, Judith, and additions to Esther/Daniel), wisdom literature (Ecclesiasticus, Wisdom of Solomon, Baruch, The Prayer of Manasseh), and apocalyptic literature (2 Esdras). While these writings were often found with Scripture, Orthodox Jews didn't consider them to be canonical. However, this isn't to suggest that they weren't read or even used in liturgical services.

Some contend that the Jews had two canons. The first canon was the Palestinian canon that's represented by the Masoretic text of the Bible, which was compiled by the Masoretic scribes between the 7th and 10th centuries A.D. This is the text of the Old Testament used by Jews, and it also is a later reproduction of what was found in the Dead Sea Scrolls. The Dead Sea Scrolls are the earliest surviving manuscripts of Old Testament texts. Therefore, our Old Testaments—when they translate into English—are translating from the Masoretic text, which corresponds to the earliest copies known to man (ca. 200 B.C.). The Apocrypha is not among the Masoretic text, so that's one reason we don't include it in our Old Testaments.

The second canon was the Alexandrian canon. Alexandria, Egypt was an epicenter of learning in antiquity. After Alexander the Great died and Ptolemy II ruled Egypt, legend has it that he had all the popular books in the ancient world translated into Greek. According to tradition in the Epistle of Aristeas (2nd century B.C.), Ptolemy had seventy Hebrew scribes translate the Old Testament into Greek—hence the name Septuagint, a name denoting the seventy scholars. The Septuagint is sometimes referenced by Roman numerals LXX, so if you ever see this in a footnote in your Bible, you'll know what it means. There's actually no evidence of an Alexandrian canon, and Philo, the Alexandrian Jewish philosopher, never indicated that the Apocrypha was ever canonical. The Jews in Alexandria may have added the books alongside the canonical writings, but this doesn't suggest that they were equal to Scripture. Since Alexandria was known for its learning, it may have very well been that those books were studied along or even used with Scripture, but not regarded as such.

APOCRYPHA—CANONICAL OR NOT?

People who grew up Catholic or Orthodox would have had these books in their Old Testaments. Both Catholics and Orthodox will argue for their inclusion in Scripture as Scripture, but there's a good reason why we don't include them as Scripture. As a matter of clarity, the Orthodox do not refer to these books as "Apocrypha," but "deutero-canonical" ("second canon"). I'll explain that more in a bit. Why don't we include these books in our Old Testaments?

Some people argue for the acceptance of the apocryphal books as Scripture based on their inclusion in the earliest codices ("books") of the Greek Old Testament (Septuagint, or LXX) that date to the 4th-5th centuries A.D. It's true that the Old Testament quotations contained in the New Testament are from the Septuagint. If you've ever compared an Old Testament reference in the New with what the Old actually says, there's a bit of a difference. For example, Isaiah 7:14 says that a "virgin" shall conceive and bear a son. The Hebrew term translated there could also be translated as "maiden" or "unmarried woman." The word denoted a young lady who hadn't been breached through copulation. However, when the Hebrew Old Testament was translated into Greek, the term inserted in the place of the Hebrew term *almah* was the Greek term for "virgin," *parthenos*—we get our word "parthenon" from this Greek term. In actuality, the Septuagint is an excellent Jewish commentary on the Hebrew Old Testament merely through its translation. Translation, after all, is interpretation.

The Apocrypha was not originally included when the Septuagint was first translated in the 3rd-2nd centuries B.C. Origen, the third-century church theologian that we've already mentioned, listed the Old Testament books in the order they appeared in the Christian codices of the Septuagint. Jerome refused to include them when he composed the Latin translation of the Bible in the late fourth century; however, after his death, they were added.

WHY WERE THEY ADDED?

The eastern churches in Asia Minor, Palestine, and Egypt kept the Jewish canon in early Christian history. While these books were included in the earliest codices that we have, some scholars believe that they were regarded not as Scripture but as ecclesiastical (church) books. To put it another way, it would be like how preachers sometimes rely on commentaries to understand the Bible. The commentary gives insight and is helpful, but it is not itself inspired.

These books were first formally recognized by the Catholic Church as "Divine Scripture" at The Council of Trent (Session IV, 1546). They were not included in the original Hebrew Scriptures, but they were declared "genuine parts of Scripture" by the Church Councils of Jassy (1642) and Jerusalem (1672). Even the Orthodox scholar, Timothy Ware, recognizes this.

> The Septuagint contains in addition ten further books, not present in the Hebrew, which are known in the Orthodox Church as the "Deuter-Canonical Books."...most Orthodox scholars at present day, however, following the opinion of Athanasius and

Jerome, consider that the Deutero-Canonical Books, although a part of the Bible, stand on a lower footing than the rest of the Old Testament.[1]

The Jewish canon was the choice of the Reformers in the 16th century.

THE APOCRYPHA'S USEFULNESS

These books do have value for understanding first-century Judaism. When the voice of prophecy had ceased, these books gave a voice to what happened between the Testaments religiously, literarily, and historically. The two books of the Maccabees detail the struggle of the Jews for religious and political freedom, and they record a heroic period of Hebrew history. These books also help us understand the spiritual, philosophical, and intellectual life of the Jews before Christ's birth.

Hebrews 11:34–38 shows a familiarity with the apocryphal books (cf. 2 Maccabees 7:1–29). Jesus was also acquainted with these books as a comparison of His sayings with them shows.

Do not store up for yourselves treasures on earth, where moth and rust consume and where thieves break in and steal; but store up for yourselves treasures in heaven, where neither moth nor rust consumes and where thieves do not break in and steal. (Matthew 6:19–20)

Lay up your treasure according to the commandments of the Most High, and it will profit you more than gold. (Sirach 29:11)

> In everything do to others as you would have them do to you; for this is the law and the prophets. (Matthew 7:12)

> And what you hate, do not do to anyone. (Tobit 4:15)

> You will know them by their fruits. (Matthew 7:16)

> Its fruit discloses the cultivation of a tree; so a person's speech discloses the cultivation of his mind. (Sirach 27:6)

Just because Christ knew about these books and even might have paraphrased them doesn't suggest that they should be canonical. After all, Paul quoted from pagan poets when he preached in Athens (Acts 17:28) and wrote to Titus (Titus 1:12). Moreover, Jude 14 quotes 1 Enoch 1:9 while Jude 9 quotes the Assumption of Moses—non-canonical writings.

THE LESSONS

With the Reformation Movement came a particular belief—*Sola Scriptura* (Scripture only). As the only guide of faith and rule of practice, yes, the Scriptures need to stand alone as the authoritative teachings of God. However, our modern obsession with Scripture only robs us of a fuller richness of faith. The Apocrypha isn't inspired, but it probably should be read so that we can be Bible students who are not wholly ignorant of New Testament institutions and thinking. The Jews read the Scriptures as authoritative, but they also had other books that were useful to them, as did the early church.

I've shown that the canonical writers of the New Testament read secular literature, and it actually helped them writing the Holy Writ. Think also about how Moses was schooled in all things Egyptian (Acts 7:22) and Daniel and his companions were schooled in all things Chaldean (Daniel 1:4–5). These great characters had secular learning, remained dedicated to God, and used their secular education in a manner to glorify God. Add to the fact that their secular education was also pagan, and it's even more impressive.

I've heard members of the church say, "All I need is the Bible." I wouldn't necessarily argue against that, but I would say that those who rely solely on the Bible are also relying on scholarship that has translated the Bible from its original languages into English so that they can only use the Bible. Reading other works related to sacred Scripture doesn't mean that we esteem them as equal to Scripture. However, as those characters in the Old Testament and the writers of the New Testament show us, secular learning can be used for God's glory. Therefore, we shouldn't disdain works that are non-canonical. I'm tremendously blessed when I read the Bible. I'm also blessed when I've read Christian works that are not divinely inspired.

FILL IN THE BLANK

1. "Apocrypha" means _____.

2. The _____ canon that our Old Testaments derive from doesn't include the Apocrypha while the _____ canon does.

3. The Orthodox Church doesn't call these books "apocryphal," but _____ which means _____.

4. _____ didn't include them in his Latin translation

of the Bible.

5. The first point in time when these books were declared Scripture was at the Council of _____ in the year _____.

DISCUSSION QUESTIONS

1. How can we read non-canonical sources and not esteem them as authoritative while, at the same time, admiring the purpose they might serve?

2. Does Jesus' use of the Apocrypha mean that all of it was inspired, or just the parts that He quoted?

3. What does the Bible's usage of non-canonical literature suggest about where we might find truth?

4. What are some things we can learn from the Apocrypha?

5. How can we make sure that we, like Moses and Daniel and his companions, use our secular knowledge to help us spiritually?

NOTES

1. Timothy Ware, *The Orthodox Church*, new ed. (New York: Penguin Books, 1993), 200.

8

JEWISH ANTIPATHY TOWARDS GENTILES

Any time you greatly love something, you're bound to dislike anything that may be a threat to it. The Jews in the Intertestamental Period had devoted themselves to fidelity to God, and in doing so, they became opposed not only to that which might threaten their religion, but also to those they perceived as posing that threat. We see the term "Gentile" in the New Testament used for everyone who wasn't a Jew. The Greek term is *ethnos*—from which we get our term "ethnic." The Gentiles and their ways had almost unseated Jewish life, but the Maccabean revolt trumped that and led to a greater focus on the Torah and the Tanakh. The result was a disdain for foreigners and their ways.

XENOPHOBIA IN ANTIQUITY

I'm going to choose to define "xenophobia" here as "antipathy to foreigners" for the purposes of this lesson. There are many reasons why one might be xenophobic, but hopefully, this will serve as a good enough foundation for our study. In Eastern antiquity, xenophobia was rather common. People were always leery of foreigners because the commonly held belief was that the foreigner may possess some magic that they may use to enchant or curse with.

Egyptian culture was famous for their xenophobia. The ancient world knew that Egypt hated strangers, and a part of the reason they did was religious in nature. Mythically, Egypt was to sacrifice strangers to their gods to ensure that rains would continue on the land so that they could reap a harvest. While the reason was religious in nature, it also served economic and social means. Unlike our modern society which tends towards secularism, ancient societies—their economies and morals—were indistinguishable from their religions. It is striking that Abraham showed hospitality to the heavenly visitors by the Oaks of Mamre in Genesis 18, especially after having recently been in Egypt. Abraham's generosity and hospitality became a point of reference for both Jewish and early Christian hospitality since he was the father of the faithful.

The Law stated that God "loves the stranger, giving him food and clothing" (Deuteronomy 10:18). Therefore, Israel was prohibited from mistreating strangers because of God's love for them (Exodus 22:21; 23:9). Foreigners were actually given equal treatment and protection under the Law in Israel (Exodus 12:49). Yet, not all people were treated equally according to Law. For example, women had rights similar to those of children and slaves, and this is seen when the men of Sodom pressed on Lot's home in how Lot offered his virgin daughters to them. Another example of this is seen in Judges when the Levite's concubine was raped by the men of the city so that he remained unharmed (Judges 19).

According to the Scriptures, Israel was to regard themselves as strangers and sojourners with God in the land of Canaan (Leviticus 25:23). Contrasting how they had been treated in Egypt as slaves, God wanted them to develop an ethic of hospitality after the manner of Abraham as a primary mode of behavior. After all, Israel knew what it was like to be a stranger in a foreign land and to be mistreated (Exodus 23:9). However, with all that happened in the Intertestamental Period, xenophobia grew towards non-Jews (Gentiles) and is perfectly attested to in the New Testament.

THE RISE OF JEWISH XENOPHOBIA

With the invasion of Hellenism in Judea and the conformity of many of the Jews to the Greek ways, those who wanted to preserve their culture became so dedicated to being Jewish (religiously and culturally) that they began denouncing strange ways and even foreign people. As we've seen, the Jews dedicated themselves to their religion and culture through the Scriptures and the synagogue. Sects arose that pursued this end as we've already mentioned. The natural response when so intently focusing on this was a disdain for all things foreign, especially when they contradicted Judaism.

In the Intertestamental Period, the view shifted from the Jews seeing themselves as God's chosen people to seeing themselves as being God's exclusive concern. The Essenes and other sects isolated themselves from the surrounding societies—similar to the Amish—and developed an attitude of superiority. Understandably, their attitude developed from what they had recently endured at the hands of the Gentiles.

> After subduing Egypt, Antiochus returned in the one hundred forty-third year. He went up against Israel and came to Jerusalem with a strong force. He arrogantly entered the sanctuary and took the golden altar, the lampstand for the light, and all its utensils. He took also the table for the bread of the Presence, the cups for drink offerings, the bowls, the golden cen-

sers, the curtain, the crowns, and the gold decoration on the front of the temple; he stripped it all off. He took the silver and the gold, and the costly vessels; he took also the hidden treasures that he found. Taking them all, he went into his own land. He shed much blood, and spoke with great arrogance. Israel mourned deeply in every community, rulers and elders groaned, young women and young men became faint, the beauty of the women faded. Every bridegroom took up the lament; she who sat in the bridal chamber was mourning. Even the land trembled for its inhabitants, and all the house of Jacob was clothed with shame. Two years later the king sent to the cities of Judah a chief collector of tribute, and he came to Jerusalem with a large force. Deceitfully he spoke peaceable words to them, and they believed him; but he suddenly fell upon the city, dealt it a severe blow, and destroyed many people of Israel. He plundered the city, burned it with fire, and tore down its houses and its surrounding walls. They took captive the women and children, and seized the livestock. Then they fortified the city of David with a great strong wall and strong towers, and it became their citadel. They stationed there a sinful people, men who were renegades. These strengthened their position; they stored up arms and food, and collecting the spoils of Jerusalem they stored them there, and became a great menace, for the citadel became an ambush against the sanctuary, an evil adversary of Israel at all times. On every side of the sanctuary they shed innocent blood; they even defiled the sanctuary. Because of them the residents of Jerusalem fled; she became a dwelling of strangers; she became strange to her offspring, and her children forsook her. Her sanctuary became desolate like a desert; her feasts were turned into mourning, her sabbaths into a reproach, her honor into contempt. Her dishonor now grew as great as her glory; her exaltation was turned into mourning. (1 Maccabees 1:20–40)

The Jews began associating Gentile behavior with God's judgment on the world, and they looked to the case of Noah as a proof of their belief. It was believed that the chief sins of the world in Noah's time were bloodshed, sexual abominations, and idolatry—all of which warranted God's judgment and were associated with paganism. The Jew believed it was better to have died than commit any of these three sins.

Gentiles, therefore, became associated with sin. Jews began avoiding them unless it was necessary. The rabbinical tractate *Avodah Zarah* (A.D. 200)—which means "strange worship"—was solely written to instruct Jews as to how they shouldn't defile themselves. For example, they could not leave livestock in Gentile inns because of the sin of bestiality. Israelite women were not to be the midwives or wet nurses of Gentiles since the mother had birthed an idolator (*Avodah Zarah* 2.1). After all, Israelite-Gentile intermingling resulted in banishment from the Promised Land and judgment from God.

Just because the Jews believed that Gentiles were to have been avoided at all costs doesn't necessarily indicate that they thought it was appropriate to go out of one's way to mistreat them. The Cairo Damascus Document found among the Dead Sea Scrolls attests to the fact that a Jew was not to harm a Gentile for wealth or gain. Jews could have interactions with Gentiles, but there were religious protocols as to how and when this was permissible. This is also not to suggest that all Jewish-Gentile relations with Gentiles were monolithic. Some sects were very stringent in their interactions with Gentiles, while others were more liberal about it. The Herodians favored Roman rule while the Pharisees didn't, as one example.

When we arrive at the New Testament, we understand many avoidances of Jewish-Gentile intermingling by the Jews (John 18:28; Acts 10:28; Galatians 2:12–14). We also understand why it was so remarkable that Jesus sat with the Samaritan woman at the well in John 4 and why there was a dispute over the distribution of food in Acts 6. The Hellenist Jews were believed to have been sell-outs because they were Jewish but with a Hellenist influence in their dress, speech, and other habits. However, when Jesus gave His Great Commission, we see that God had not favored only Jews. He brought salvation to all nations.

THE LESSONS

We must be careful that our response to something doesn't go so far that we forget who God wants us to be. We as Christians are to have an identity that reflects Christ. Sadly, things occur that move us to respond to them, and in so doing, we sometimes chip away a piece of our Christian identity. Allow me, if you will, to use one of American Christianity's sacred cows as a point of reference.

Our national security is something vitally important to us. I confess that I want to be safe, and I want to live in a safe homeland. I also don't wish to invite any harm to my wife and children and the rest of my family. In the interest of my own level of comfort, I will speak against receiving Syrian refugees because of the threat that they may pose to me and mine. However, I read about how the Hebrew Christians "joyfully accepted the plundering of [their] goods" (Hebrews 10:34). As the passage went on to state, they knew that they had "a better and an enduring possession" that awaited them in heaven.

You may not struggle with this as I do. Maybe you want to keep the refugees out or let them in. One is a view of prudence while the other is purely compassionate. Is there a middle ground? I don't know. Which will I focus on—my fears or my faith? Sometimes fear—an emotion given to us by God for our own protection, I'm convinced—allows you to make a right decision. Also, who can go wrong with extending compassion? Even if I'm harmed out of being giving and compassionate to another, surely God wouldn't judge me for what might be a poor judgment by human standards.

I wish I had the answer. I know some will state it one way or the other, but this is an issue I struggled with articulating a view on. I see both sides of the coin. However, I'm not entirely convinced that prudence is the best course always, nor is compassion. What I must be careful not to do is allow my heart to swerve from following God's standard of righteousness and holiness. The Jews gave a lot of attention to the Law, yes. However, they seemed to have overlooked those passages in the Law that spoke about how they should treat the stranger. Paralleled to this has been a Christian insistence on protecting unborn life and not granting same-sex marriages—views derived from God's Word. Yet, some of these same Christians are warmongers and refuse to allow their Christianity to inform them when it comes to compassion and hospitality. It only goes to show that none of us are 100% consistent with the expression of our views.

FILL IN THE BLANK

1. All who were non-Jews were called _____.

2. _____ culture had a reputation for mistreating foreigners.

3. The Israelites were to be as _____ and _____ in the land of Canaan.

4. The rabbinical tractate _____ was dedicated to explaining Jewish-Gentile interactions to protect the Jew from defilement.

5. The _____ Jews were disliked because they were believed to have been sell-outs.

DISCUSSION QUESTIONS

1. Since the Jews were so dedicated to the Law and missed obeying the commandments regarding strangers, what might this suggest about how we study the Bible today and what we might miss in studying God's Word? Are we also guilty of picking and choosing how to follow the Bible?

2. When we consider what all the early Christians were willing to endure for their faith in Christ, do we find that we are too comfortable in America to care to suffer as they did?

3. Are the Scriptures always black and white, or is there sometimes a gray area that we often miss?

4. The Israelites were commanded to keep themselves apart from the people of Canaan, and at times to destroy them. They were also commanded not to mistreat the stranger in their land. Discuss the reasons for the differences that applied to how they were to act towards others.

5. One group of Jews believed the Hellenist Jews to be sellouts because of their acceptance of some parts of Greek culture. Do we let cultural differences become a barrier to how we treat other Christians? How can we be careful to separate spiritual differences from cultural ones?

6. What are some ways we can show hospitality to others? How can this help us strengthen and care for our brethren or reach out to non-Christians?

9

THE EMERGENCE OF ROME

Despite the Jews having a natural dislike of foreigners, there were times when alliances with them were advantageous to the Jews. Christ Himself and the faith that bears His name would be born during the days, not of the Greeks, but of the Romans. We continue to see the prophecy of Daniel 2 played out before us, and it would be during this particular kingdom that God would establish His everlasting kingdom and rule. However, though Rome will be spoken of here in generous terms, we must remember that Rome was not always a friend of the Jews or Christians. There were times when Rome persecuted both, but Rome in and of herself was the medium through which the Gospel would be spread to God's glory.

EARLY ROME

The Roman people's history stretches back all the way to the eighth century B.C. when Rome was merely a village. During the reign of Caesar Augustus—who was emperor when Christ was born (Luke 2:1)—the poet Vergil composed his epic, *Aeneid*. The poem presents the origins of Rome beginning after the city of Troy was defeated by the Greeks when Aeneas the Trojan voyaged to Rome to establish the Roman people. Initially a monarchy, Rome became a republic around 509 B.C. and remained as such until 27 B.C.

By the fifth century B.C., Rome had started spreading throughout the entire Italian peninsula, and by the third century, Italy was under complete Roman dominance. A significant turning point for Rome came during the third and second centuries. Rome was continually expanding its territories, and two rival competitors were Greece and Carthage (Egypt). The wars with Greece were called the Macedonian Wars (214–148 B.C.), and the wars with Carthage were known as the Punic Wars (264–146 B.C.). Rome took the Corinthian peninsula in 146 B.C., thus ending the Macedonian Wars while simultaneously destroying Carthage the same year. Winning these wars resulted in the emergence of Rome.

THE JEWISH ALLIANCE WITH ROME

Hearing of the advantages of being friends with Rome, the Jews believed that an alliance with them would be helpful in recovering the Promised Land from the Greeks (1 Maccabees 8:1–2, 12–13). By this time, Greece had terribly enslaved Israel, so the Jews sent a few delegates to Rome to form an alliance. Rome was elated to receive the friendship of the Jews because Israel was a strategic location that could prove profitable to Rome. The association was recorded on bronze tablets and sent to Jerusalem (1 Maccabees 8:23–32; cf. *Antiquities of the Jews* 13.9.2). This Jewish-Roman treaty occurred in 161 B.C.

A considerable period of Jewish-Roman history began in 63 B.C. when Pompey had taken possession of Jerusalem. The Psalms of Solomon was the first Jewish writing that expressed hatred for Rome after Pompey entered the Holy of Holies. In this book, the author stated the belief in the coming of a righteous Messiah-King like David, Israel's greatest king. This Messiah-King would deliver the land from foreign oppression and occupation of the pagans.

This was also a tumultuous time for Rome because two of her titans, Julius Caesar and Pompey Magnus, would later battle one another in the civil war. Before they fought one another, Caesar, Pompey, and Marcus Crassus—the richest man in Roman history and a Roman general—were aligned and dominated Roman politics. Crassus was catapulted to notoriety when he defeated the slave rebellion led by Spartacus in 71 B.C. Crassus captured 6,000 slaves and had them crucified along the Via Appia so that it served as an example to all who defied Rome. Crassus was later appointed as governor of Syria, during which time he attempted to expand Rome's power by fighting the Parthians (Iranians). Crassus' campaign failed, and he was killed in battle. During the alliance of the three, Pompey had married Caesar's daughter, Julia. Pompey hated Crassus, and Crassus hated Pompey. Julia, Pompey's wife, died during childbirth that was induced by shock when she thought her husband had been killed in battle. With Crassus and Julia now dead, nothing linked Pompey and Caesar anymore. Pompey aligned himself with a conservative group of the Senate and began contending for leadership of Rome against Julius Caesar that led to civil war in 49 B.C.

When civil war broke out, those in charge in Israel changed alliances with whomever was in charge of Rome to their own benefit. The Jews won Caesar's favor after the civil war ended. Pompey had fled to Egypt and was assassinated there, so Caesar went to Egypt. He was blocked in Alexandria, but Jewish reinforcements arrived to aid Caesar in defeating his enemies. From that moment, Caesar looked favorably upon the Jews. He granted them a reduction in tribute and exempted all Jews from military service. This would have pleased the Jews for economic and religious reasons because the Roman military participated in Rome's paganism since its religion was inseparable from its government.

Herod was made tetrarch of Judea along with another by Caesar's general, Mark Antony. Later, however, the Senate declared Herod king of the Jews in 40 B.C., and Herod won the kingdom in 37 B.C. Jesus was born during his reign (Matthew 2:1), and Josephus informs us that Herod died between 4–6 B.C. (*Antiquities of the Jews* 17.8.1). This time span is given because Herod had all male children two years old and younger murdered (Matthew 2:16).

HOW ROME AIDED CHRISTIANITY

Since Christianity was born in the days of the Roman Empire, we can see after reflecting upon Rome just how it aided the spread of Christianity. The first way it helped the spread of Christianity was through being so religious itself.

> The quality in which the Roman commonwealth is most distinctly superior is in my opinion the nature of their religious convictions. I believe that it is the very thing which among other peoples is an object of reproach, I mean superstition, which maintains the cohesion of the Roman state. (Polybius *Histories* 6.56)

> In piety, in devotion to religion,...we have excelled ever race and every nation. (Cicero *Response to the Soothsayers* 9.19)

Rome's piety paved the way for the spread of Christianity in that the Empire was naturally disposed to religion, so when the Christians preached Christ as the only God, it would have taken hold for those seeking true religion.

Because Rome was religious, Christians borrowed from the imperial language to tell the story of Christ. Since Caesar Augustus—heir of Julius Caesar—ended all wars and ushered in the Peace of Rome (*Pax Romanum*), he was lauded as a hero of Rome. One inscription reads of him,

> Since the Providence which has ordered all things and is deeply interested in our life has set in most perfect order by giving us to Augustus, whom she filled with virtue that he might benefit mankind, sending him as a Saviour [*Sōtēr*], both for us and for our descendants, that he might end war and arrange all things, and since he, Caesar, by his appearance, surpassing all previous benefactors, and not even leaving to posterity and hope of surpassing what he had done, and since the birthday of the god Augustus was the beginning for the world of the good tidings [*euangélion*] that came by reason of him...

In Vergil's epic, as well as his other works, he explicitly "prophesied" about the reign of Caesar Augustus as an anticipated reign of glory (*Aen.* 6.791-7). Vergil's epic was published in 19 B.C., so by the time of Luke's Gospel, the notion of Caesar Augustus being a Roman "Messiah" was firmly implanted in the Roman mind (cf. *Ecl.* 4.4–52). Augustus' reign was synonymous with peace and prosperity, but Jesus' reign in the kingdom of God would solidify the very concepts of peace and prosperity.

A final way that Rome helped the spread of Christianity was through its infrastructure. Roman travel was rather simple, and that proved beneficial to the early Christians who traveled regularly.

THE LESSONS

Sometimes we may think that alliances with certain groups or individuals may be pertinent at one time or another. Looking at the Jewish dislike of the Greeks, we might even say that Israel chose the lesser of two evils. However, the relationship that the Jews forged with the Romans was a relationship that didn't cause the Jews to compromise. Though the relationship grew from mutual benefit into hatred over time, it was initially beneficial to both parties.

There are passages such as 1 Corinthians 15:33 that state the importance of selecting good company. This is a lesson that we teach our children. Yet, the relationship of the Jews with the Romans was such in the beginning that it freed the Jews from Grecian oppression and Hellenistic customs. In a manner of speaking, the alliance with Rome brought the Jews a liberty that allowed them to be Jewish.

Our having relations with those outside of the faith aren't necessarily evil in themselves. However, had the relationship proven to be a burden to Jewish culture, we might suspect that the Jews would have avoided it. The Jewish alliance with Rome didn't suggest that the Jews condoned all of Rome or her ways. Sometimes things aren't as black and white as they appear.

A second lesson that I see here is that God uses even the least likely of means for His own sake. Just look at how, through His divine foreknowledge, God put the birth of Christianity in the Roman Empire. There are many more aids to the spread of the faith that could be listed, but those that I've listed show a wisdom of God that we might just underestimate from time to time.

The good thing about Rome that is absent in our own time is a general piety. As were all ancient civilizations, ancient Rome was religious, but our culture is growing increasingly secular. Rome called on idols that didn't really exist, while our society calls on intellectualism. Our task may be harder in spreading the gospel given the sinful nature of the West, but solutions are always sought to life's greatest problems. God often provides those answers.

FILL IN THE BLANK

1. Jesus was born during the reign of Caesar _____.

2. Jesus was born when _____ was king of Judea.

3. Two of Rome's titans, _____ and _____, were engaged in civil war.

4. _____ took possession of Israel and entered the Holy of Holies.

5. The work _____ is the first Jewish work that reflects a Jewish hatred for Rome and a wish for a Messiah-King like _____.

DISCUSSION QUESTIONS

1. When are relationships with those of different faiths advantageous to a Christian and when are they disadvantageous?

2. How do world events impact Christianity? Should Christians be concerned about them?

3. What role does a culture's government play in religion?

4. Discuss the events of the time that helped Jesus and the early church to accomplish their missions.

5. Compare the teaching of the Gospel in our culture with other cultures that you may be familiar with, perhaps through mission work that you or your congregation is involved in. What are some challenges that you may have in the area that you live that others may not face? What are some advantages

of your area? How can recognizing these strengths and weaknesses of our culture help us to be more effective in teaching others about Jesus?

10

THEOLOGICAL DEVELOPMENTS

Not only were some institutions and sects in the New Testament relatively novel to Judaism, but some doctrinal stances became more developed between the testaments as well. Particularly, one of the most developed doctrines from the Intertestamental Period was that of angels and demons. Not much information about them exists in the Old Testament, but by the New Testament, we read about demon possession and the works of Satan at large. This is not to entirely suggest that the Old Testament is silent on this issue, because it isn't (cf. 1 Kings 22:19–23). However, there just isn't as much written in the Old Testament about this operation in the celestial realm as there is in the New.

ANGELOLOGY

Perhaps the most developed doctrine that emerged during the Intertestamental Period regarded angels and demons, including Satan. Before turning to the development of this subject in the Intertestamental Period, let's first look at our Bibles to see what can be understood of them from there. A lot of our modern interpretation of the subject and the New Testament teachings on the topic were born from this period of time.

From the Old Testament we first meet, not the devil or Satan, but the serpent who deceived Eve. From our New Testament, we're informed that Satan was the serpent in the Garden of Eden (Revelation 12:9; 20:2), but ancient audiences may not have understood this before the period between the testaments. Angels are created beings (Psalm 148:2, 5) who were present when God created the earth (Job 38:1–7). Among angels were systems of rank with the highest level being the archangels. Our Bibles only note Michael as the archangel (Jude 1:9), but the Jews believed in seven archangels.

> I am Raphael, one of the seven angels who stand ready and enter before the glory of the Lord. (Tobit 12:15)

> And these are the names of the holy angels who watch. Uriel, one of the holy angels, who is over the world and over Tartarus. Raphael, one of the holy angels, who is over the spirits of men. Raguel, one of the holy angels who takes vengeance on the world of the luminaries. Michael, one of the holy angels, to wit, he that is set over the best part of mankind and over chaos. Saraqael, one of the holy angels, who is set over the spirits, who sin in the spirit. Gabriel, one of the holy angels, who is over Paradise and the serpents and the Cherubim. Remiel, one of the holy angels, whom God set over those who rise. (1 Enoch 20:1–8)

The number seven in Jewish numerology symbolized perfection because God created the earth in seven days. Nevertheless, the cherubim and seraphim are the only two other angelic orders of which we know from our Old Testaments, but there were more orders listed in the Intertestamental Period. There were, in addition to these three already listed, the Ophannim, angels of power, principalities, and other powers of the earth (1 Enoch 61:10). Their appearance was also described.

> And his body was white as snow and red as the blooming of a rose, and the hair of his head and his long locks were white as wool, and his eyes beautiful. And when he opened his eyes, he lighted up the whole house like the sun, and the whole house.... his nature is different and he is not like us, and his eyes are as the rays of the sun, and his countenance is glorious. (1 Enoch 106:2, 5–6)

> And there appeared to me two men, exceeding big, so that I never saw such on earth; their faces were shining like the sun, their eyes too (were) like a burning light, and from their lips was fire coming forth with clothing and singing of various kinds in appearance purple, their wings (were) brighter than gold, their hands whiter than snow. (2 Enoch 1:6)

Some early Jewish art depicts angels as not having wings whenever they manifested as humans such as with the angels that visited Abraham by the Oaks at Mamre in Genesis 18 (cf. Genesis 19:1).

After humanity's fall, cherubim guarded the Garden of Eden. The throne of God is elsewhere depicted as resting upon this class of angels (2 Samuel 22:11; Psalm 18:10). When the Ark of the Covenant was made, two cherubim were placed on each side to cover the Ark on which God's presence dwelt (Exodus 25:18–22), which explains the statement that God dwelt between the cherubim (Psalm 80:1;

99:1; Isaiah 37:16). From Isaiah 6:1–3, we see a caste of angels called Seraphim ("fiery ones") attending to God.

SATAN AND DEMONS

Satan was believed to have once been a cherub that rebelled against God, and Isaiah 14:12–15 was a passage utilized to explain his rebellion.

> How you are fallen from heaven, O Lucifer, son of the morning! How you are cut down to the ground, You who weakened the nations! For you have said in your heart: "I will ascend into heaven, I will exalt my throne above the stars of God; I will also sit on the mount of the congregation On the farthest sides of the north; I will ascend above the heights of the clouds, I will be like the Most High." Yet you shall be brought down to Sheol, To the lowest depths of the Pit.

Satan is also mentioned in Job, but given the mysterious nature of Job, clarification needs to be made. Despite the attempt of scholars to arrive at a date, no one actually knows the dating of the book of Job. When we see Satan mentioned in Job 1:6, the definite article appears before it. Therefore, in Hebrew, *satan* is not a proper name. The Hebrew term *satan* means "adversary." The text literally reads that "the adversary" came among the sons of God—a designation used of angels. At times, even God is referred to as a *satan* (Numbers 22:22, 32). After the exilic period, we see more of Satan, the first mention of him being in Zechariah 3:1–2 and again in 1 Chronicles 21:1. Otherwise, there isn't much else to go off from the Old Testament about Satan.

The most famous tale of the rise of demons among first-century

Jews and Christians was held to have originated in Genesis 6:1–4. The language of this passage posits the sons of God (angels) as taking human wives. Then, in v. 4, this passage says that there were giants on the earth (NKJV). We could say that the sons of God were giants based on the description of 2 Enoch 1:6 mentioning angels that were "exceeding big." Another suggestion is that the term *nephilim* could also mean "fallen ones" since they came from heaven. The only other time this Hebrew term is used appears in Numbers 13:33.

Mirroring the passage from Genesis 6, 1 Enoch 6–11 retells the story in greater depth. However, 1 Enoch—without apology—reads not "sons of God," but "angels." Those angels all numbered to 200, and their offspring are called "giants." The angels eventually turned to gross sin and began killing men upon which the prayers of men ascended to heaven. Uriel is sent by God to warn Noah to prepare for what was to come. Raphael bound Azazel—possibly another name for Satan (cf. Leviticus 16:8, 10, 26)—and cast him into the darkness until the great judgment at which time he would be thrown into the fire (cf. Matthew 25:41). "And the whole earth has been corrupted through the works that were taught by Azazel: to him ascribe all sin" (1 Enoch 10:8–9). The angels that led this effort were to have been bound until the judgment at which time they too would be cast into the fire. This narrative sheds light on two New Testament passages—

For if God did not spare the angels who sinned, but cast them down to hell and delivered them into chains of darkness, to be reserved for judgment. (2 Peter 2:4)

And the angels who did not keep their proper domain, but left their own abode, He has reserved in everlasting chains under darkness for the judgment of the great day. (Jude 1:6)

These passages reflect the belief that the offspring of the mating between the angels and humans resulted in the birth of demons. I do believe that the early Christians accepted 1 Enoch, not as Scripture, but as a significant work. Jude actually cited 1 Enoch in Jude 1:14–15. However, that no more makes all of Enoch inspired, divine truth than Paul quoting from pagan prophets or other books of the Old Testament using sources we no longer have access to (cf. Numbers 21:14; Joshua 10:13; 2 Samuel 1:18; 1 Kings 11:41).

THE LESSONS

What are we to make of a doctrinal development that seems to have taken place without inspired Scripture? Remember that people of old were primarily oral, whereas we're more literary and visual. A lot of teachings that were later recorded can be said to have been preserved through oral teaching. After all, the oral teachings of the rabbis were claimed to have existed from the time of Moses himself. Someone may say that oral transmission is like the telephone game that we play and that the story is subject to misconstruing as it's transmitted. Yet, that would be us binding our own limitations on ancient people. They learned differently than we do, and they had a better capacity for oral retention than we do in our age of technology. Think about it: some of our parents or grandparents can recall a relative's phone number, whereas I have to rely on the contacts in my cell phone. That's just one generation of difference.

Some early Christians regarded 1 Enoch as inspired, but it ultimately didn't live up to the criteria of the New Testament canonization process, which included a writing's apostolicity, its conforming to the rule of faith, and the universal appeal it might have enjoyed in the church throughout the world. The Ethiopian church, however, preserved it in their own canon. First Enoch didn't belong to the

Apocrypha, but to the pseudepigrapha ("false writing"). It's a writing that gives us a window into first-century Judaism and Christianity, so if we who seek to restore New Testament Christianity want to continue doing such, we might be well served by reading what the early Christians also read—not thinking of it as inspired, but as useful.

FILL IN THE BLANK

1. The Jews believed that there was not one, but _____ archangels.

2. In the Bible, the only archangel ever named was _____.

3. The Hebrew term *satan* means _____.

4. An earlier name for Satan was _____ as it's seen in the book of Leviticus.

5. The Jews understood the narrative in _____ as telling of the creation of demons.

DISCUSSION QUESTIONS

1. Since some books of the Bible quote from secular works, how can we determine how much of a secular work may contain divine truth if at all?

2. Does the Scriptures' usage of secular works alter the way we view the Scriptures' message at all, and if so, how?

3. Could we argue for an oral transmission of what 1 Enoch says based on its claimed historicity, or must we argue for an Intertestamental Period origin?

4. This lesson discusses how the New Testament gave more information about angels, demons, and Satan than God's peo-

ple of the Old Testament had. What are some other areas that spiritual understanding was different for New Testament Christians than for the Jews who only had the divine revelation of the Old Testament?

5. How do you regard using books that are not part of our biblical canon to help us understand spiritual matters?

11

RELIGIOUS EXPECTATIONS

It may seem that the previous and current chapters are a bit disjointed. However, the reader will likely find, as I explain below, a better correlation than might have been initially assumed. What people believe about doctrine, good, and evil directly impacts how they tend to view many issues. For example, we who believe in the God of the Bible have adopted a certain ethic that coincides with God's holiness. As a part and parcel of that ethic, we tend to view issues through our religious convictions (e.g. abortion and same-sex marriages). The Jews' outlook on angels, Satan, and demons led them to assign to their oppressors the power of Satan and his demons, while at the same time assigning their victories to the power of God and His angels as they might have worked on their behalf. Yet, the spiritual war that was taking place had a culmination, and it would require a special person or people (Messiah) enabled by God to do His will on earth as it is in heaven to bring about the end result, the kingdom of God.

MESSIANIC EXPECTATIONS

The term "Messiah" in Hebrew (lit. "Anointed") was indicative of one who had been anointed and was often applied to religious (Leviticus 4:3, 5) and political (1 Samuel 2:10) leaders of Israel. "Messiah" was also used of even King Cyrus of Persia (Isaiah 45:1). Generally speaking, the term was used of anyone who was chosen by God for a particular office. During the Intertestamental Period, the "Messiah" of God—an eschatological ("end-time") figure—as we think of Jesus became more developed. The Psalms of Solomon—a writing known to early Christians that dated to the first or second century B.C.—gives descriptions of the Messiah that would later become Jesus.

> And he (shall be) a righteous king, taught of God... the anointed ("Messiah") of the Lord. (17.32)

> And he himself (will be) pure from sin, so that he may rule a great people. (17.36)

> And (relying) upon his God, throughout his days he will not stumble; For God will make him mighty by means of (His) holy spirit, And wise by means of the spirit of understanding, with strength and righteousness. (17.37)

When Jesus came, the majority of Jews believed the Messiah would have been a political, military king who addressed the woes of the nation.

There was no unanimous outlook on God's coming Messiah, however. The group at Qumran, among whom were the Essenes, looked for more than one figure and in their documents portrayed his coming with a final war to be followed by a divine blessing and banquet. Another variation of Messiah was that of the Levitical Messiah. This title emphasized the priestly function of Messiah, which according to some in the Qumran community took precedence over the political role.

> For to Levi the Lord gave the sovereignty, and to Judah, and to me also with them, and to Dan and Joseph, that we should be for rulers. Therefore I command you to hearken to Levi, because he shall know the law of the Lord, and shall give ordinances for judgment and sacrifice for all Israel until the completion of the times of Christ, the High Priest whom the Lord has declared....And worship we his Seed, because He shall die for us in wars visible and invisible, and shall be among you an everlasting king. (*Testament of Reuben* 6)

A fully developed understanding of the divine Messiah, as opposed to the secular ruler, appears in 2 Esdras 11-13 and 1 Enoch 37-71. Therein, the vision is likened to and references that of Daniel, thus drawing the comparison between the two references (2 Esdras 12:11; cf. Daniel 2:44). Depicted in 1 Enoch 37-71 is another description of Messiah, which contains occasional references to him as a Son of Man. The description in these passages represents the Messiah as one who is akin to the apostle John's Word, or Logos (cf. John 1:1–3, 14). He was pre-existent and regal as the Son of Man. However, his character was that of a servant (Isaiah 53; cf. Matthew 20:28). The service of Messiah to humanity was to reconcile them to God.

The Jews did not comprehend the service of Messiah as well as they did the political function of Messiah. The reason for this may have been their subservience to the Romans during Christ's time. They would have readily sought a monarchical rule whereby the Messiah crushed God's enemies and made peace for them, thus restoring the kingdom to Israel (cf. Acts 1:6). However, the peace that Jesus gave was with God (John 14:27). The lack of political rule that the Jews desired, along with the fact that He was crucified (cf. Deuteronomy 21:23), were key elements to the Jews' rejection of Jesus as Messiah. Paul said this was a stumbling block to his fellow countrymen (1 Corinthians 1:23). A prophet like Moses and Elijah were also titles sometimes ascribed to Messiah (Deuteronomy 18:15–19; Malachi 4:5–6); however, these were rare instances when compared to the previous ones mentioned. Nevertheless, while many groups emphasized one or a few aspects of the Messiah's persona, Jesus fulfilled them all in some way.

KINGDOM EXPECTATIONS

Many of the writers of this time used Isaiah 11:1–9 as the basis for their belief that the kingdom of God was wholly of the world (cf. John 18:36) and everlasting, so when they wrote about God's kingdom, they portrayed it in such a way.

> And then shall all the righteous escape, And shall live till they beget thousands of children, And all the days of their youth and their old age Shall they complete in peace. And then shall the whole earth be tilled in righteousness, and shall all be planted with trees and be full of blessing. And all desirable trees shall be planted on it, and they shall plant vines on it: and the vine which they plant thereon shall yield wine in abundance, and as for all the seed which is sown thereon each measure (of it) shall bear a thou-

sand, and each measure of olives shall yield. (1 Enoch 10:17–19)

Blessed be God who lives forever, because his kingdom lasts throughout all ages. (Tobit 13:1)

And Thy goodness is upon Israel in Thy kingdom.... And the kingdom of our God is forever over the nations in judgment. (*Psalms of Solomon* 5.18; 17.3)

Isaiah 65:17–22 also led these writers to see the messianic kingdom as brief and was to have been replaced by an eternal kingdom accompanying a new creation (2 Enoch 32:3–33:2; cf. 2 Esdras 7:26ff).

One thing was sure, the coming kingdom was equated with the defeat of Satan and his rule—"Then this kingdom will appear throughout his whole creation. Then the devil will have an end" (*Assumption of Moses* 10). Because of the theological developments of the devil, angels, and demons, Satan occupied a prominent role in the woes of the world and specifically to those that afflicted God's people. With Satan meeting his end, God's people would be sorrow free and happy because their enemies who were under Satan's control would no longer exercise dominion over them. The defeat of Satan coincided with the defeat of Israel's mortal enemies, and the Dead Sea Scrolls states this in the War Scroll:

The first battalion being armed with lance and shield and the second with shield and sword to slay through the judgment of God and to vanquish the line of the enemy of God's might, to exacts retribution for their wickedness upon all nations of vanity, and the kingdom shall be of the God of Israel, and He shall do valiant deeds through the saints of His people. (1QM 6:5–6)

Even passages from the Old Testament lead to this interpretation. When the Jews reflected upon David's everlasting kingdom (2 Samuel 7), they thought David's descendant would rule a literal kingdom that was of the world. This promise was compounded by the promise being extended through David's son, Solomon (1 Chronicles 28:5–7). Even later Jeroboam was rebuked for thinking that he could disrupt God's plan by removing the kingdom from the dynasty of David (2 Chronicles 13:8). In the purview of Isaiah, the nation appeared physical (Isaiah 52:7). The passage of the valley of the dry bones in Ezekiel was taken as a restoration of the nation of Israel, accompanied by an outpouring of God's Spirit as mentioned in Joel 2:28–32. All of these would lead to an absolute intellectual belief that is seemingly represented but not exactly fulfilled as the Jews expected.

THE LESSONS

There's a warning here. We know the outcome of the religious expectations as they regarded the Messiah and the Kingdom of God. Many people followed Jesus, but many others didn't because of those expectations. Chief among a large number of detractors was the religious leaders of the day. Many Pharisees and others simply didn't see God's anointed in Jesus of Nazareth. This leads to something that may make you a bit irritated with me. American Christianity is as such that American Christians cling to their guns and Bibles, if not something else. I don't see how clinging to our guns is a part of our religion. Clinging to our Bibles? Yes. However, I fail to understand how anything else could be put beside a Bible, whether it is a gun, flag, standard, politician, or other element. Our faith is what will endure and nothing else.

Too often, we strive to make the United States God's country. I'm as familiar as most are with our country's religious heritage, but we must also concede that some of our founders were deists who actually believed the Bible to have been rubbish (e.g. Thomas Paine). The Bible guided their wisdom in the founding of our country, however, the country was not meant to have been a theocracy, but a republic.

I say all that to say that Israel's political expectations for the Messiah were a part of what led so many to reject Jesus as Messiah. They wanted a warring military leader who would be king and not earthly spiritual leadership. What does it say of us when we as American Christians seem to place our hope so much in a politician from one particular party, perhaps forgetting the idea that we may sing on a Sunday morning that, "This world is not my home, I'm just a passing through…"? Let us all strive to do the best we can for our nation (cf. Jeremiah 29:7), while at the same time not confusing our civil rights with our Christianity.

FILL IN THE BLANK

1. The term "Messiah" means _____.

2. "Messiah" was used of _____, _____, and even _____.

3. The _____ community believed that Messiah would have been a Levite, thus stressing the priestly function of God's anointed.

4. The Jews of Jesus' time believed that the kingdom of God would be of the _____.

5. The coming kingdom was equated with the defeat of
_____.

DISCUSSION QUESTIONS

1. When so many theories abound about doctrine, how can one decide what's right or how to formulate a balanced view?

2. How can politics lead to a misreading of the Bible?

3. How can we as Christians balance our faith vs. doing good on earth through being involved in the political process?

4. Many Jews missed seeing the Messiah because he was not what they were expecting. What are some examples of spiritual truths missed by the religious because they are contrary to what they expect of God or the church? What are some measures that we can take not to miss spiritual truths that could be contrary to our own pre-conceived expectations?

5. Do you believe the Jews were truly looking for the Messiah? What were they hoping for with his arrival? Today, we also believe in the coming of Jesus. How do our attitudes toward this coming compare or contrast with that of the Jews looking for the first coming?

12

FALSE MESSIAHS

When we understand the Jewish expectations of the Messiah, we clearly understand how they might be led astray. It isn't that the misleading was intentional, but these people were looking towards a Messiah that they hoped would restore their nation to its former glory and relieve the oppression of foreign rule. When people are looking for hope, they search for it as a thirsty man seeks water in a desert. Hope is one of those realities outside of ourselves that keeps us going. When people lose hope, what do they have left but memories, if even that? Of course, the worldliness of their expectations is nearly akin to that of Americans today who always seek a messianic politician to restore prosperity and morality to our country. We're not different than they were. However, we have the hindsight of history—some of it divine and some secular—to remove the obstacle from us and point the way to Christ our Lord.

We have hindsight to see the truth of the light of Jesus, but they had only the prophecies. If you're anything like me, there are parts of the Bible that are nearly impossible to understand. I might suggest that some prophecies were that way for the Jews back then. They based their expectations off of what they could understand, and this was a people who knew war and what a political, military Messiah could bring to the table.

DESPERATE FOR HOPE

During the Intertestamental Period, the Jews closely followed the prophecies believing that God's Messiah was close to coming to them. I once read somewhere that the scroll of Daniel was the most abundant writing found in the Dead Sea Scrolls. We may presume that those of that community closely followed the prophecies within Daniel in eager anticipation of God's Messiah coming to establish God's eternal kingdom. Therefore, it became very comfortable when individual men rose up to follow them while believing they were from God and were ready to do His will.

After Christianity was born, the apostles drew large targets on their backs by preaching Jesus Christ as God's Messiah after He had been put to death by the Romans at the instigation of the Jews. As the Sanhedrin heard the apostles and were plotting to kill them, Gamaliel addressed the entire council with these words—

> And he said to them: "Men of Israel, take heed to yourselves what you intend to do regarding these men. For some time ago Theudas rose up, claiming to be somebody. A number of men, about four hundred, joined him. He was slain, and all who obeyed him were scattered and came to nothing. After this man, Judas of Galilee rose up in the days of the census, and drew away many people after him. He also perished, and all who obeyed him were dispersed. And now I say to you, keep away from these men and let them alone; for if this plan or this work is of men,

it will come to nothing; but if it is of God, you cannot overthrow it—lest you even be found to fight against God." (Acts 5:35–39)

These two names—Theudas and Judas of Galilee—were figures outside of the narrative of our New Testaments who led insurrections only to be quashed by the authorities. People followed them believing them to be God's Messiah, but as their revolutions were quelled, the people learned otherwise.

Of Theudas, we know nothing other than what the Bible says of him. Since Gamaliel named him first, we may presume that he led his revolt before Judas. Josephus mentioned a person named Theudas, but he came much later than the one mentioned here according to Josephus' chronology.

Judas the Galilean led his revolution during the census of Quirinius, which would date to sometime in A.D. 6 (Luke 2:1; *Antiquities of the Jews* 20.5.2). What would have made Judas easier to follow would have been Isaiah's prophecy about Galilee—

> Nevertheless the gloom will not be upon her who is distressed, As when at first He lightly esteemed The land of Zebulun and the land of Naphtali, And afterward more heavily oppressed her, By the way of the sea, beyond the Jordan, In Galilee of the Gentiles. (Isaiah 9:1)

The prophecy might have been interpreted as the person would have been from Galilee, but the way it was used in applying to Jesus was that His ministry began there (Matthew 4:15–16). However, the census was what prompted Judas to revolt, and the Jews were understandably on board with his actions since to him taxation was equivalent to slavery. Judas had Pharisaic beliefs, so he had a supportive audience and strong constituency to his credit.

Other false messiahs revolted that are not named in the New Testament. When we understand that men arose claiming to be from God and were proven wrong, we understand the religious leaders of Jesus' day being hesitant to affirm His messiahship. They had seen it all before and were not prepared to be taken for fools again.

MISSING GOD'S HOPE

Jesus grew up in a culture in which false messiahs had set the tenor of Jewish expectation. When Christ arose and didn't fit this particular mold, he was rather rapidly rejected by a considerable number of Jews, although there were others who believed Him to be God's Messiah. Regardless, Christ did God's will according to the divinely established decree of heaven. Before He died, he gave His apostles a hint into just how things would be after His death.

Jesus had told His disciples that even after Him people would arise claiming to be the Christ (Matthew 24:5). The episode of Gamaliel from Acts took place in A.D. 35. However, sometime from A.D. 52–59—some suggest A.D. 55—an Egyptian revolutionary did the same, and he and Paul were thought to be one and the same (Acts 21:38).

> But there was an Egyptian false prophet that did the Jews more mischief than the former; for he was a cheat, and pretended to be a prophet also, and got together thirty thousand men that were deluded by him; (262) these he led round about from the wilderness to the mount which was called the Mount of Olives, and was ready to break into Jerusalem by force

from that place; and if he could but once conquer the Roman garrison and the people, he intended to domineer over them by the assistance of those guards of his that were to break into the city with him, (263) but Felix prevented his attempt, and met him with his Roman soldiers, while all the people assisted him in his attack upon them, insomuch that, when it came to a battle, the Egyptian ran away, with a few others, while the greatest part of those that were with him were either destroyed or taken alive; but the rest of the multitude were dispersed every one to their own homes and there concealed themselves. (*Wars of the Jews* 2.13.5)

There were even groups that preceded the Egyptian uprising that Josephus records. Before and after Christ, we see revolutions led by men who amassed small armies to take on Rome and liberate Judea. They were still seeking the earthly kingdom that they perceived was the fulfillment of God's promises. Long after this time, the first person to explicitly be called "Messiah" was Simon Bar Kokhba who in A.D. 135 led another revolution against Rome. Later rabbis referred to him as Bar Kosiba, which meant "son of a lie." The Jewish conception of Messiah had not come. Sadly, though, many Jews believed Christ to have been a false messiah because of just how different His ministry was from their own beliefs of who Messiah should be.

THE LESSONS

Someone once gave me a piece of advice that I've used in many scenarios. I've used this piece of advice when deciding to leave secular work to enter the ministry. I've used this piece of advice when deciding to leave one congregation to go work with another. I've given this advice to people who were thinking about marrying someone else, or entering a relationship. Here it is—"Are you running *to* something or *from* something?" This is an important question to answer. If you're running to something, then by all means move to it with assurance. If you're running from something, you may very well settle for what is not God's plan for your life.

The Jews were running from Roman oppression. Who can blame them? However, in running from what they disdained most, they ran to something that was not everlasting. Something that was not God's plan. Something that perpetuated letting them down and the emotions that follow being let down. Why? Because they failed to see God's will as it was revealed in His Scriptures. Their hearts had been self-seeking rather than God-seeking. They were blind in sight and dull of hearing.

Too many churches run from false teaching and practices, only to practice a conservatism that means doing nothing and playing it safe all the time. They refuse to step outside of their buildings and carry their Christianity into their communities. Because they've occupied a piece of land for so long, they believe that they have a presence in the community when all they do is take up room. They never try anything because they have a "we've tried it before and it didn't work" mindset. Should we avoid false teaching? Yes. But not at the expense of doing God's will, and His will includes more than showing up and worshiping Him. His will for us is that we be lights. If people don't look to your church for a light to the community, you're failing at being God's people where you are.

Another lesson central to this chapter is that when people seek hope, they often look to a person who they think brings that hope with them. Jesus is really the only one ever to fulfill that, and blessed were those who saw Him and served Him in the here and now. Many churches are filled with good preachers, but those preachers shouldn't be mistaken for the actual Messiah. Theudas, Judas, and the Egyptian might have been charismatic leaders who persuaded the people easily. Perhaps it was for this reason that God saw His people as sheep. Sometimes sheep are easily led to their own destruction. Elders must stand up and shepherd the flock. More often than not, the preacher is the pastor even though he doesn't wear that title.

FILL IN THE BLANK

1. The Dead Sea Scrolls had more copies of the book of _____ than any other Old Testament prophecy.

2. Judas the Galilean led his rebellion because of the census of _____.

3. _____ was mistaken of being the Egyptian that led a revolt.

4. The first person to have been called Messiah was _____.

5. Later rabbis referred to him as the son of a _____.

DISCUSSION QUESTIONS

1. What are some things that the church and Christians run from that leads them to embracing something that's not as fulfilling?

2. How might we, in addition to studying the Scriptures, discern God's will?

3. How should leaders be regarded according to the Scriptures?

4. Do you think you would have been able to recognize Jesus as the Messiah if you only had the information the Jews had?

Would it have been difficult? Do you think it is easier for us since we have history and the writings of the New Testament? Why or why not?

5. Are people who follow false teachers today any different from those who followed false messiahs? Are they searching for hope they believe the false teachers provide? What efforts can we make to reach those who are following false teachers?

13

WHY THE JEWS REJECTED JESUS

The false Messiahs, most of whom led revolutions against occupying Rome, had set the tone for what the Jews believed their Messiah was to do. Of course, prophecies from the Law and Prophets aided their misinterpretation as well as wishful thinking. When Jesus arrived on the scene in His ministry, He was bound to do God's will. However, people perceived God's will as one thing while He revealed it to be another. Many followed Christ faithfully, acknowledging that He was God's true Messiah, but still others rejected Him because of their own preconceived notions. They were not open to correction, and this was why they rejected Christ as God's Messiah. They saw it going one way when God had other plans.

PREPARING THE WAY OF THE LORD

Before the Messiah came, there was to be one who would prepare the way of the Lord. The person of John the Baptist was prophesied in Malachi 4:5. Within this passage is the fact that Elijah would be sent with the purpose of turning the hearts of God's people. An appropriate commentary on John's person as Elijah is given in the Intertestamental writing where this passage is almost quoted verbatim in Sirach 48:10-11. Therefore, John's purpose was to return before the coming of the Messiah to reconcile God's people to Him, and this was what John's baptism of repentance did.

The ministry of Elijah was to comfort God's people. The description of Elijah's ministry was perceived to be one that brought reconciliation in the preparation for the Lord's ministry. Accompanying this Elijah was a Mosaic-like prophet (cf. Deuteronomy 18:15; cf. John 1:21; 6:14; 7:40). Others supposed that this prophet was a particular prophet from the past, such as Jeremiah (Matthew 16:14).

Since John the Baptist was likened to Elijah, we must ask ourselves how the two were alike. Several comparisons may be made. First, they both endured a period of preparation—Elijah at the Brook Cherith and John in the wilderness (1 Kings 17:3; Luke 1:80). Second, they dressed alike in modest clothing that would have been worn by the poor of their respective days (Matthew 3:4; 2 Kings 1:8). Third, they preached sharp, short messages (Matthew 3:7–12; 1 Kings 17:1). Finally, they had powerful foes—Elijah had Jezebel, and John had Herodias and Herod Antipas.

When Moses and Elijah appeared with Jesus at His Transfiguration, the thought of Peter, James, and John would have been a recognition of the final age. Luke's account of the transfiguration (Luke 9:28–36) mentions Jesus speaking of His "departure;" which in Greek was *exodos*. The Exodus was associated with the Feast of Booths, so when Peter asked to build "tabernacles" (KJV), he had in mind a new Mosaic-like deliverance. John's duty, as many believed from the Scriptures and in him, was that he prepare the way of the Lord, which he did.

FINDING MESSIAH

The gospel according to John gives us a wonderful glance into the acceptance and rejection of Jesus. Shortly after the baptism of Christ by the Baptizer, Jesus began amassing disciples. The Baptizer pointed others to Christ, and one of those who had been following John the Baptist was none other than Simon Peter's brother, Andrew. Upon being led to Christ, Andrew went to Simon Peter and exclaimed, "We have found the Messiah" (John 1:41). A few verses later, Jesus called Philip to follow Him, who in turn found Nathanael and said, "We have found Him of whom Moses in the law, and also the prophets, wrote—Jesus of Nazareth, the son of Joseph" (John 1:45).

No doubt they had heard the rabbis expound upon the Law and the Prophets to prepare the minds of the people for the coming Messiah. The passage from Moses that Philip likely had in mind came from Deuteronomy 18:18—"I will raise up for them a Prophet like you from among their brethren, and will put My words in His mouth, and He shall speak to them all that I command Him." Some of the passages from the prophets that he might have had in mind would have included Isaiah 4:2; 7:14; 9:6; Micah 5:2; Zechariah 6:12. After His resurrection, Jesus would use the Law of Moses and the Prophets to explain to His apostles all things concerning Himself (Luke 24:27).

Upon meeting Jesus, Nathanael exclaimed that Christ was the Son of God and the King of Israel (John 1:49). Two passages from the Old Testament illuminate these titles. Of the Son of God, Psalm 2:7—a messianic psalm—told of God begetting His Son, something that John later includes in John 3:16. Of the King of Israel, two passages address this title.

> The Lord has taken away your judgments, He has cast out your enemy. The King of Israel, the Lord, is in

your midst; You shall see disaster no more. (Zephaniah 3:15)

Rejoice greatly, O daughter of Zion! Shout, O daughter of Jerusalem! Behold, your King is coming to you; He is just and having salvation, Lowly and riding on a donkey, A colt, the foal of a donkey. I will cut off the chariot from Ephraim and the horse from Jerusalem; The battle bow shall be cut off. He shall speak peace to the nations; His dominion shall be "from sea to sea, And from the River to the ends of the earth." (Zechariah 9:9–10)

In each of these passages, the King of Israel is depicted as removing Israel's enemy from them, bringing peace, and ruling the world. As Nathanael exclaims this of Christ, he isn't incorrect, but he does misunderstand the nature of Jesus' mission.

Some time later, Christ fed 5,000 upon which Jesus' own apostles acknowledged that He was the Prophet who was to come into the world (John 6:14). Their understanding of the Prophet merged with that of a king, so in the very next passage, they wanted to take Him and make Him king by force, but Christ withdrew from them (John 6:15). Later, they asked Christ what they must be doing to do the works of God (John 6:28). This might have been a reflection of their desire to make Him a king by force, so they might have been actually asking what their part would be in partaking of another revolution. Should they amass soldiers? Should they gather weapons? What should they do to be doing God's works? Christ then began turning their minds to who He was (John 6:29–34), but they sought from Him a sign (cf. 1 Corinthians 1:22). Jesus in effect was telling them that He was the sign they sought. All they needed to do was to believe in Him.

After teaching them many things about God's will, we read, "From that time many of His disciples went back and walked with Him no more" (John 6:66). They stopped following Jesus because they didn't see in Him the political, military ruler that they had come to expect. He couldn't have been Messiah because Messiah was to have done ABC, while this Jesus only wanted to preach a spiritual message that is not of this world.

THE LESSONS

Some people only ever see what they want to see. I fear that we are guilty of this very thing. We study the Bible through certain lenses, which isn't altogether wrong. Yet, sometimes we only see what we want to see and do not account for the whole counsel of God. For example, I've heard brethren make the statement that "when two or more are gathered together, Jesus is with them." This statement is usually made when there's low attendance at some function or worship service. Yet, the context in which that passage appears has nothing to do with how people use it. Jesus said this after explaining how to deal with a sinning brother, so the contextual meaning of the passage was that if one were put out of the fellowship of the church, Jesus would agree as long as two or three agreed on the point (Matthew 18:15–20).

One Sunday morning, the high school class was combined with the college class I was teaching in Bible study. Their teacher became ill and couldn't make it. One teen boy asked, "If denominationalists have the same Bible as we do, why are they wrong and we are right?" I replied by stating that they're not wrong on everything, just as we're not right on everything. However, the problem comes in when people use the Bible as a motivational book where they cherry-pick passages that give them the warm fuzzies. For example, "I can do all things through Christ who gives me strength" (Philippians 4:13). A football coach may use this passage and say, "Christ says we can do everything through Him, so we're gonna go out and win this football game!" That's not at all what Paul meant. Another example is, "I know the plans I have for you, declares the Lord, plans to prosper you and not harm you, plans to give you a hope and a future" (Jeremiah 29:11). People say, "This is what God says to me!" Well, God actually said it to the Jews whom He would send into Babylonian captivity. You're not a Jew, and you're not being sent into Babylonian captivity.

Sometimes well-meaning Christians and preachers use the Bible this way, thus divorcing it from its context and imposing a meaning on it that God has not given it. People who use the Bible this way see only what they want to see. The Jews, who had built an iron-clad idea of Messiah, had done the same. They saw only what they wanted to see and missed the entire point. Even when Christ appeared to explain it to them, they were so close-minded that they refused to hear how it actually was. Hopefully, all of us are open to reason when it comes to seeing something from a different perspective—"The first one to plead his cause seems right, until his neighbor comes and examines him" (Proverbs 18:17).

Thankfully, however, Peter and the apostles came along to preach the gospel in Acts 2. Many had gotten it wrong, but God sent His messengers with the good news. They had another chance. Many accepted that second chance. We too have the opportunity to right what we've wronged by studying God's Word afresh and learning from it rather than reading our preconceptions into it. Let us strive to do this which is pleasing to God.

FILL IN THE BLANK

1. The one who prepared the way of Messiah was to have been like the prophet _____.

2. The person who fit this forerunner status for Jesus was
   _____.

3. _____ led Simon Peter to Jesus.

4. The title that Nathanael used of Christ suggested that
   He was to have been a military leader. That title was
   _____.

5. Some of the disciples wanted to take Jesus and make him
   _____ by force.

DISCUSSION QUESTIONS

1. To what degree should we be open-minded and to what degree should we not be?

2. Does pointing out our weaknesses as Christians suggest that
   something's wrong with the church?

3. How can we discipline our minds not to misapply Scriptures?

4. Many Jews stopped following Jesus when they realized he
   wasn't the Messiah they were hoping for. Are people today
   guilty of only following Jesus as long as he is the Savior they
   want him to be? Can you think of examples?

5. What have you learned from this study of the Intertestamental Period that you didn't know before? Has it deepened your
   understanding of spiritual matters? If so, how?

6. The Jews expected certain things out of the Messiah, but we
   read warnings in the Bible that "my thoughts are not your
   thoughts, neither are your ways my ways, declares the Lord"
   (Isaiah 55:8). How can this verse apply to the Jews who expected certain things that were not part of God's plans? How
   can this verse apply to people today who seek to understand

God by human thought and judgments? If we don't think as God or have the same ways as God, then can we understand him? If so, how?

www.ingramcontent.com/pod-product-compliance
Lightning Source LLC
LaVergne TN
LVHW021402080426
835508LV00020B/2420